The Desktop Style Guide

THE DESKTOP STYLE GUIDE

James Felici

BANTAM BOOKS
NEW YORK · TORONTO · LONDON · SYDNEY · AUCKLAND

THE DESKTOP STYLE GUIDE
A Bantam Book/December 1991

Interior Design by Nancy Sugihara
This book was produced by Pageworks, Old Saybrook, CT

ISBN 0-553-35445-0

Published simultaneously in the United States and Canada

Bantam Books are published by Bantam Books, a division of Bantam,
Doubleday Dell Publishing Company, Inc. Its trademark, consisting of the
words "Bantam Books" and the portrayal of a rooster, is Registered in U.S.
Patent and Trademark Office and in other countries. Marca Registrada,
Bantam Books, 666 Fifth Avenue, New York, NY 10103.

PRINTED IN THE UNITED STATES OF AMERICA

0 9 8 7 6 5 4 3 2 1

Contents

CHAPTER 2

Typographic Style   27

CHAPTER 3

Special Characters   59

CHAPTER 6

Preparing an Electronic Manuscript   95

Introduction

Desktop publishing has turned millions of people into typesetters. Not long ago, a few thousand professionals at expensive computer terminals set everyone's type—they were experts for hire. But today, if you use a word processor or a page makeup program, typesetting and typography are a part of your job. If you're a writer, editor, secretary, graphic designer, word processor, or production artist, you have to be the typographic expert.

This is a book about typographic style, and I've written it for today's new generation of typesetters. Its goal is simple: to answer your day-to-day questions about how pages should look. It contains a smattering of copy-editing guidelines and a smidgen of design advice, but mainly it's about type and the style of printed pages. When you follow the basic rules in this book about how type should be set and how pages should look, many of your documents will virtually design themselves.

I created this book as a quick reference, one to keep on your desk next to your dictionary. When you have a question, the *Desktop Style Guide's* table of contents and detailed index will steer you quickly to just the information you need. And that information is concise—what you need to know and do, and no more. You don't have to read it cover to cover, you can just dive into the middle. (The chapters are sequential, though, and it does make a thorough typographic tutorial when read from front to back.)

Most of the book is a straightforward parade of facts and advice, logically organized for easy use. You may never need everything that's in this book, but you'll find it easy to access the information you *do* need.

Because publishing is a group effort, the last chapter departs from format to advise you on labor-saving ways to prepare an electronic manuscript. It shows how you can prepare a formatted document that can be printed on any computer and in any program. It shows how you can generically format your manuscripts to save time in editing, typesetting, design, and page makeup. It shows how you can prepare documents that can be typeset at the push of a button. And it shows how you can change a document's design in minutes without tedious reformatting. This is the only chapter that's best read in its entirety.

Such a small book can't answer all your questions, especially about matters of manuscript form, language, and usage. For this reason, I recommend the following books as in-depth sources to complement this one.

The Chicago Manual of Style, The University of Chicago Press, Chicago, IL

Words Into Type, Prentice Hall, Inc., Englewood Cliffs, NJ

Hart's Rules For Compositors and Readers, Oxford University Press, Oxford, England

Pocket Pal, International Paper Company, Memphis, TN

The first three are style guides for book production, because book publishers seem to be the most prodigious style guide producers. Of them, only *Hart's Rules* deals primarily with type and typesetting (although some of its British typographic conventions are at odds with standard American practice). *Pocket Pal* is a brief overview of the entire graphic arts production process.

I've written this book as a companion volume to William Strunk and E. B. White's classic, *The Elements of Style* (Macmillan, New York, NY), which in less than a hundred pages teaches a lifetime of lessons on how your text should read. As it is a guide to content, this is a guide to form. I hope this little volume will serve you equally well.

James Felici
Fontès, France

Typographic Basics

The language of modern typography is a melange of antiquated terms dating from the days of Gutenberg, some nineteenth-century printing vernacular, and a smattering of current computer jargon. While foreign to most people, it makes perfect sense and is consistent within its own context. The realm of typographic measurement, in particular, is a world apart from centimeters and inches. This chapter covers the basic concepts of typography and is a primer for learning how to speak in "typographese."

Typographic Measurements

Typographic measurements are based on two types of measuring units: *absolute units* and *relative units*.

Absolute Measuring Units

Absolute units in typography are fixed and unchanging. The standard absolute units, akin to feet and inches, are called picas and points. One pica is subdivided into twelve points.

The standard American pica measures .16604 inch, or slightly less than ⅙ inch. Desktop publishing programs, in particular those using Adobe System's PostScript, Apple Computer's QuickDraw, or other compatible page description languages, have rounded off the value of the pica to exactly ⅙ inch. This may cause some measuring inconsistency between work you may have set using commercial typesetting equipment in the past and new work you're creating now with desktop computers. The discrepancy between the old and new systems amounts to less than 3 points over the width of an 8½-by-11-inch page. However, with the increasing use of desktop-driven typesetting equipment, this is less of a problem.

Inches and millimeters are often used to describe page dimensions, but line lengths are typically expressed in picas and points, and line spacing and the size of the type itself are typically expressed in points. In general, word processing and page makeup programs ask you to specify one measuring system in which to work. Select picas and points, as the size of these units are best suited for the scale in which you'll be working.

Measuring Type

The *point size* of type is roughly equal to the distance in points from the top of the tallest letter in a typeface's alphabet (typically the ascending lowercase letters such as *b* or *l*, or the height of the capital letters) and the lowest-reaching letters (typically the *j* or *y*). This measuring scheme dates back to the days of handset type, when each letter was cast on its own metal block. The height of the block itself created the space between lines of type. The height of a capital letter is typically about ⅔ of its point size, but this varies from typeface to typeface.

The best way to measure type is with a clear acetate measuring gauge, which displays type at various sizes. You lay this gauge over your type to see which size best matches your printed sample. Because of variations in typeface design, these gauges may be more or less accurate. But with common typefaces, you can be 100 percent accurate at text sizes, and accurate within a few points at larger display sizes.

Absolute Measurement Notation

There are a number of ways to write pica and point measurements. Often, single primes represent picas and double primes express points, just as they are used to express feet and inches or minutes and seconds. For instance,

9′6″ equals 9 picas, six points

Periods are also used to separate picas and points, but be careful not to confuse these with true decimals, which are often used to express distances measured in points only. Sometimes when using a period as a separator, a zero is added before single-digit point values to reduce confusion. Hence,

9.6 picas *or* 9.06 picas	*equals*	9 picas, 6 points
12.11 picas	*equals*	12 picas, 11 points

Some desktop publishing programs use a less confusing syntax consisting of the pica and point values separated by a *p,* which stands for picas. These expressions are typed without any spaces. So,

9p6	*equals*	9 picas, 6 points
12p11	*equals*	12 picas, 11 points

The equal sign (=) is also often used to denote picas, so you may see a 12-pica line length specified as 12=.

Relative Measuring Units

Relative units are based on the size of the type you are currently using. The size of the type establishes the size of each unit. Their dependence on the size of the type establishes a proportional relationship between the space or distance expressed in these units and the type itself. When defined in relative units, a proportional relationship between two typeset characters remains constant at any point size—type and space grow and shrink together proportionately.

The *em* is the basic relative unit of typography, and its value is equal to the point size of the type in which it's used. It was originally based on the width of an uppercase *M,* but this character in most current typefaces is typically not a full em in width. When you're using 14-point type, an em equals 14 points. In 36 point type, an em equals 36 points. A 3-em paragraph indent in a passage of 10-point type will be 30 points deep.

An *em space* is a unit of typographic distance equal to one em. The concept of the em and the em space only make sense in the context of a specified point size or in describing general size or space relationships.

An *en,* in turn, is equal to one-half em, so an en in 14-point type equals 7 points. An en is approximately equal to the average width of a lower-case letter, so approximated distances (line lengths, for instance) are sometimes expressed in ens. As with ems, they are often used as spacing elements, or *en spaces.*

A *thin space* is usually equal to about one-half of an en (or one-quarter of an em), but the value of the thin space can typically be defined in a typesetting or page composition program. Thin spaces are often defined to be the same width as a standard word space as created by the space bar on the keyboard. The width of a thin space is constant and predictable. Word spaces are typically stretched and squeezed by typesetting software to fit type into specified measures.

The *figure space* is the same width as the numeric characters of a typeface. All numeric characters (0 through 9) in text typefaces have the same widths so that numbers in tabular matter will automatically align. Figure spaces are used in lieu of numerals to help align numbers. For instance, in the following example, figure spaces have been added between the dollar sign and the number in the first entries to get the dollar signs in the top and bottom lines to line up:

$$\begin{array}{lll} & \$ & 89.50 \\ & & 145.50 \\ & & 918.25 \\ \text{Total} & \$ & 1153.25 \end{array}$$

Many of the smallest typographic adjustments, such as those used in *kerning* (adjusting the spaces between letter pairs; see Kerning later in this chapter) are measured in fractions of an em. A kerning relationship between two letters that is expressed in fractions of an em will remain constant at any point size in which those letters are set. Typesetting programs vary in how finely they subdivide an em, but for most purposes, units of $1/100$ of an em are more than precise enough. A $1/1000$ of an em reduction in space between two letters is too fine to make a significant difference, if not too small to see. This would be the equivalent of moving inch-tall characters together or apart by less than $1/10$ of a point ($1/720$ of an inch).

Character widths—the widths of each typeset letter—are also measured in relative units. In a system that uses 100 units per em, an *e* might be 54 units wide, while an em dash would be a full 100 units wide. Because a computer fills lines of type by counting the cumulative widths of the letters on each line, the use of relative units to describe character width provides a measurement scheme that functions at any point size. In a *monospaced typeface,* such as Courier and other typewriter faces, all characters have the same width. In *proportionally spaced typefaces*, the widths of letters vary according to the design of each character. The characters in proportionally spaced typefaces are easier to read because they've been designed using the letters' natural proportions.

The Baseline and Other Basic Reference Points

Type is measured and described using standard points of reference. The most fundamental of these is the *baseline*, the imaginary line upon which most characters appear to sit. *Leading* (pronounced *ledding*), the distance between successive lines of type, is measured from the baseline of one line of type to the baseline of the preceding line. When a designer creates a page grid for laying out a document, the positions of various text elements (such as title, byline, first line of text, etc.) are designated by the locations of their baselines.

Desktop publishing programs typically handle text as though it existed within a box, and the edges of this box are used for alignment. At left and right, these edges coincide with the left and right margins of the text block, so using them as alignment guides poses no problem. But the top and bottom edges of this "bounding box" are not a consistent distance from the baseline of the first or last lines of type within that box. The larger the type within the box or the wider the line spacing used in it, the more white space there will be between the edge of the box and the type itself. You'll always have more precise and predictable control over the placement of your text if you align text blocks according to the positions of their baselines, rather than by the edges of their bounding boxes.

The positions of all text elements on a page, then, should be described by specifying baseline-to-baseline (or simply *base-to-base*) measurements. This is often written in shorthand, such as:

24' b-b   *means*   position the first baseline of this text element 24 points below the last baseline of the preceding one.

When you use illustrations, tables, or figures with captions, the distance between the last line of a caption and the first line of a text block below it should also be specified as a baseline-to-baseline measurement. The same goes for the positions of titles, bylines, footnotes, and so on.

Rules (such as hairlines) also sit on baselines, just like text. For example, in type that's been set 16 points base-to-base below a rule, the distance up from the baseline of the text to the bottom of the rule is 16 points. Likewise, when a rule has been set 16 points base-to-base below that text, the distance from the bottom of the rule to the baseline of the text is again 16 points.

This system of measurement is also used with non-text objects, such as photographs, where the bottom edge of a photo is construed as its baseline.

When text begins at the top of the page, with nothing else above it, the first baseline of text is measured from the top (trimmed) edge of the page.

Parallel to the baseline run other reference lines (see Figure 1.1). The *ascent line* is the imaginary line to which all of the ascending lowercase letters (such as *d* and *l*) in a typeface reach. Close by is the *capital line*, the height to which all of the capital letters in a typeface reach. In texts that use capitals and lowercase, symbols such as the copyright and trademark symbols *top-align* along the ascent line, like helium balloons that hug this imaginary ceiling. In all-capital texts, the capital line becomes the top-alignment guide.

The *median line* marks the line to which unascending lowercase letters reach. The height of the *x* is used as the benchmark for this measurement. Thus the term *x-height* refers to the distance between the baseline and the median line, or to the height of a typical lowercase letter.

Finally, and least useful of all these horizontal guidelines, is the

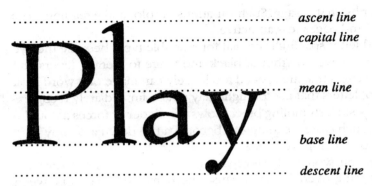

ascent line
capital line

mean line

base line

descent line

Figure 1.1
These five horizontal lines represent the basic alignment points in a line of type. The ascent line represents the ceiling reached by the typeface's tallest characters, commonly the ascending lowercase letters, as shown. The capital line is commonly slightly lower than the ascent line (the difference is unusually great in the face used for this illustration).

The mean line is an indicator of the face's *x-height*—the height of its lowercase letters. The baseline is the line on which all characters appear to sit, and the descent line is the depth to which descending lowercase letters reach. The distance between the ascent line and the descent line—measured in points—is approximately equal to the point size of the type.

descent line, the imaginary line down to which the descending characters of a typeface (such as *j* and *g*) reach.

Type Color

It's easier and more pleasant to read a page of type when the rhythm of the letters and words and the spaces between them is balanced and consistent. This consistency must exist from word to word and line to line. The lines themselves have to be leaded to preserve this balance in the vertical direction. When letter, word, and line spacing are consistent and balanced, the page of text is said to have good overall *color.*

If letter and word spacing is too tight, lines appear too dark. If loosely set, the lines will appear too light. If an entire paragraph is set too loose or too tight, its color will contrast with that of other paragraphs on the page. Such variations in color make reading more difficult and pages less attractive.

Good letter spacing is crucial for readable type, because the eye relies on an even rhythm of black and white to identify letters and words. Letters that are spaced too loosely can make one word look like two; letters that are too tight may not be immediately recognizable. Any such stumbling block slows the reader or forces a double-take. In such cases, reading can become a trip down a bumpy road instead of a well-paved street.

In general, word and letter spacing can be programmed to provide even spacing overall. But because the perceived spaces between letters are also determined by the relative shapes of those letters, perfect letter spacing sometimes requires making spacing adjustments on a case by case basis.

Once the horizontal spacing of the type has been set, the vertical spacing of the lines—their *leading*—can be set to match. If lines are leaded too tightly, the reader's eye can get lost when traveling from the end of one line to the beginning of the next. The band of white space between lines has to be wide enough to provide an easy path for the reader's eye to follow. The longer the line, the wider this path should be. Tightly leaded lines also make a page too dense and gray-looking, which can discourage readers.

If lines are leaded too loosely, the page can seem to break up into horizontal stripes. Where letter and word spacing has been tightly set, this problem is further exaggerated, because the color of the type in the horizontal direction is so much darker than in the vertical direction.

Hyphenation and Justification

A typesetting program sets type in lines by using a process called *hyphenation and justification* (or *h&j*). *Justification* is the process of filling lines with type, and hyphenation is a tool toward this goal. (Note that the word *justification* in this sense refers to fitting type into lines regardless of how the margins are specified. In terms of the h&j program, all lines are justified, whether they have ragged margins or justified margins.)

To h&j text, a typesetting program counts the cumulative widths of the letters it's placing on a line. When it determines that the next whole word will not fit within the specified measure, it then has three options for how to fill the line: (1) stretch word and/or letter spaces, (2) squeeze word and/or letter spaces, or (3) hyphenate the word that won't fit. Typically, hyphenation is used in conjunction with some modification of the spaces on the line.

In ragged margin copy it's not important to completely fill the line with type, so any extra space on the line is placed at the end. In such settings, you can allow the program to hyphenate and to vary word and letter spacing in order to control how ragged the margin will be (see Aesthetic Rags this chapter).

The h&j program is also affected by other variables you can control, including kerning and tracking adjustments. How to use all these controls is discussed later in this chapter.

Point Size and Line Length

Proportion is the essence of typography, and the most fundamental typographic relationship is the ratio of point size to line length. If the point size you choose is too large for the line length, or *measure*, awkward letter and word spacing may occur. In such a line, there are not enough word and letter spaces in which the program can distribute leftover space, so spacing becomes irregular even if almost every line is hyphenated.

If the point size you choose is too small for the line length (or the line length is too long for the point size), the page will seem very gray. The reader's eye may also stray from the correct line when moving from one line to the next.

The proper balance of type size and measure also depends on the typeface you choose. For example, sans serif and condensed type-faces should be set in narrower measures than normal-width serifed faces, which were designed for text.

The following formulas provide an easy way to approximate proper line length. Individual cases will vary slightly according to the typeface and spacing you choose, but these basic ratios will always get you close to a harmonious balance.

You can judge the balance of point size and line lengths by the numbers of words that will fit within the measure:

Number of words for serifed faces:

Minimum	Optimum	Maximum
5–6	9–10	14–16

Number of words for sans serif faces:

Minimum	Optimum	Maximum
5–6	7–8	10–12

You can also estimate the proper line length by comparing the size of the type (expressed in points) to the measure (expressed in picas) using the following technique:

For serifed faces:

Minimum line length in picas equals the type size in points (e.g., 10-point type over a 10-pica measure)

Optimum line length in picas is about twice the type size in points (e.g., 10-point type over a 20-pica measure)

Maximum line length in picas equals three times the type size in points (e.g., 10-point type over a 30-pica measure)

For sans serif faces:

Minimum line length in picas equals the type size in points (e.g., 10-point type over a 10-pica measure)

Optimum line length in picas is about one-and-a-half times the type size in points (e.g., 10-point type over a 15-pica measure)

Maximum line length in picas equals twice the type size in points (e.g., 10-point type over a 20-pica measure)

Leading

Leading is the vertical distance between lines of type as measured from the baseline of one line of type to the baseline of the line above it.

The tightest normal leading for text is called *solid*. In this instance, the leading value is the same as the point size in use, for example, 12-

point type on 12 points of lead. Solid leading is commonly used in newspapers, where space is tight and columns are narrow.

More standard leading adds one extra point of space (e.g., 12 on 13), which creates more open and readable text. One extra point of lead works well in narrow measures and measures up to the optimum range specified above. In the optimum line-length range, leading is typically set at 120% of the point size—thus 10 on 12, or 12 on 14 (or 14.5).

A handy way to gauge appropriate leading is to divide the number of picas in your measure by your type size measured in points. The number this division yields, rounded off to the nearest half-point, is the amount of extra leading you should use. For 12-point type on a 30-pica measure, this division yields the value 2.5, so the type should be set 12 on 14.5. This formula is only a rule of thumb, but it gets you very close to the proper measurements.

In certain circumstances, you can set type with negative leading, where the leading is less than the point size of the type. This shouldn't be done in upper-and-lowercase text, but it's often useful with all-caps or caps-and-small-caps, as well as in display type, where tight spacing is the rule rather than the exception.

Word and Letter Spacing

Your composition program should rely almost exclusively on altering word spaces to justify type. You can't alter letter spaces very much without compromising readability.

Serifed and sans serif typefaces should be spaced differently. Serifed types are inherently more readable because the serifs help to differentiate letters. Sans serif faces should be spaced more loosely so that individual characters stand out more clearly against the page.

Type composition programs enable you to specify the range in which letter and word spaces can be manipulated during justi-fication. This range is defined by the *optimum* space for which the program should strive, the *minimum* width to which it can squeeze the spaces, and the *maximum* amount it can stretch them. The following values are good guidelines for use in text with justified margins, where 100% represents a normal setting:

Letter Spaces

	Minimum	Optimum	Maximum
Serifed faces	95%	100%	110%
Sans serif faces	100%	100%	110%

Word Spaces

	Minimum	Optimum	Maximum
Serifed faces	75%	100%	125%
Sans serif faces	90%	100%	125%

For ragged margins, word and letter spaces shouldn't be allowed to vary as widely as in justified type, and minimum, maximum, and optimum letter space values should all be 100%. For word spaces, use 100% as both a minimum and optimum and 115% as a maximum.

Remember that altering word and letter spacing deviates from the natural spacing of the typeface. These variations should be viewed as a necessary evil when setting justified type. The character fitting of each face was determined by the designer of that face, and the designer should know best how that type should be spaced. The light touch, in other words, is the right touch when modifying word and letter spacing.

Kerning

Kerning is the adjustment of spaces between individual pairs of letters to compensate for any incongruence in their shapes, which can cause gaps or pinched spaces between letters. Letters with diagonal shapes (A, v), concave shapes (x, K), convex shapes (O, c), and letters with overhanging parts (T, Y) most commonly create kerning problems.

In body text, kerning should be left to your program's *automatic kerning* utility, which makes adjustments between letters as it composes the text. It does this by referring to a table of kerning pair adjustments stored in the font itself or within the program. You can add pairs to these tables and assign appropriate values to ensure consistent spacing for all character combinations. Better yet, you can buy premade kerning tables for your typefaces, which will save you this painstaking and time-consuming task. Professional-quality kerning tables typically contain well over 1,000 kerning pairs.

Automatic kerning based on kerning tables works fine for text sizes. In display type, however, kerning problems are much more

Excited

Unkerned

Excited

Over-kerned

Excited

Correctly kerned

Figure 1.2
Kerning adjustments compensate for irregular spacing caused by the shapes of neighboring letters. In the upper sample, the text appears without any kerning adjustments, and the spacing between letters is much looser in the first half of the word than in the second.

The middle sample is over-kerned. The amount of white space between every letter pair has been made equal, but the overall effect is clearly wrong, with some pairs of letters looking very pinched.

The bottom sample has been correctly kerned to create the *effect* of even spacing. The *Ex, xc,* and *ci* pairs have been tightened so an even rhythm of alternating black and white prevails throughout the word.

obvious and distracting. Some *hand kerning* is necessary in point sizes over 24-point if you want professional results.

As Figure 1.2 shows, the object of kerning is not to nestle characters as closely together as possible, but rather to provide even and consistent spacing from letter to letter and word to word. When kerning by hand, start with adjustments of about 1/50 em. Although programs typically allow you to use far finer increments, 1/50 em should be precise enough for most occasions, with 1/100 em adjustments for fine corrections.

Don't kern numbers in tables. Numerals in text faces all have the same character widths so they'll align neatly into columns when used in tables. Kerning numbers would disrupt this alignment.

In display type and even in text, though, it may be useful to add some kerning pairs that include numerals into the kerning tables your program uses. These should include combinations in which the narrow number *1* appears, as well as numerals appearing next to punctuation, especially commas and periods. If you have added numeral kerning pairs to your kerning tables, turn the automatic kerning off when setting tables.

Tracking Control

Tracking is the overall tightness of the type. When you adjust the tracking within a passage of text, you globally and evenly affect the word and letter spacing by reducing or enlarging the amount of space each letter and word space occupies on the page. The shapes of the letters remain the same, they just appear to nuzzle closer together or spread farther apart.

The most common reason to adjust tracking is to compensate for the apparently looser spacing of type in large point sizes. In other words, large type needs to be spaced more tightly than small type to set with the same apparent degree of tightness.

Programs that offer automatic tracking control typically allow you to set point-size thresholds at which the tracking of type will automatically be tightened. Logical thresholds with the amount that tracking should be tightened are: 14-point (2%), 36-point (5%), 54-point (10%), and 72-point (15%). With these degrees of adjustment, type set at all sizes will appear to be spaced equally tightly, as seen in Figure 1.3.

Natural   *12-point* *normal*

Natural   *18-point* *–2%*

Natural   *36-point* *–5%*

Natural   *54-point* *–7%*

Natural   *72-point* *–10%*

Natural   *72-point* *normal*

Figure 1.3
The tracking of type should be tightened as the point size increases. This prevents large type from looking too loose. Here, the progressive degrees of tightening (shown as percentages) yield the same sense of spacing across a range of point sizes. The samples get tighter but they all appear to share the same spacing. The 72-point sample at the bottom is set with the same tracking setting as the 12-point sample at the top, but it looks much looser.

Hyphenation and Line Breaking

Type composition programs offer three kinds of hyphenation:

logic-based, in which the program deduces hyphenation mathematically

dictionary-based, in which the program refers to an internal dictionary

manual, in which you add hyphens yourself

In general, dictionary hyphenation is more accurate, but logic-based (or *algorithmic*) hyphenation is faster. Many programs first use a dictionary to determine hyphenation, and if the target word isn't found, they use a logic program as a backup.

All type composition and text processing programs enable you to build your own hyphenation dictionary to supplement the program's automatic facility. These *exception* or *supplementary dictionaries* should be circulated at intervals among all members of a workgroup to assure consistent hyphenation.

All computer hyphenation should be proofread and badly hyphenated words should be added to the exception dictionary. Hyphenation programs have the most difficulty with technical terms, jargon, proper names, and product names.

Sometimes the same word is hyphenated differently according to how it's used:

pro-ject as a verb, *proj-ect* as a noun
pro-duce as a verb, *prod-uce* as a noun
de-sert as a verb, *des-ert* as a noun
pre-sent as a verb, *pres-ent* as a noun or adjective
pro-gress as a verb, *prog-ress* as a noun

The correct hyphenation of these words can only be verified by a dictionary.

Computer programs distinguish between *hard hyphens* (keystroked characters) and *soft* or *discretionary hyphens* (introduced by the computer to break lines). Hard hyphens are fixed characters in a text; soft hyphens disappear when the text is re-ragged. When hyphenating manually, always use your program's soft hyphen command to break words at the desired places.

The basic rules of hyphenation are:

- Words of less than six characters should not be hyphenated.
- At least two letters should precede the hyphen.
- At least three letters of a hyphenated word should be carried to the next line.
- A word containing a hard hyphen should be broken only at that hyphen; no word should be double-hyphenated.
- No more than two consecutive lines should be hyphenated (three are permissible in narrow columns).
- The last word of a paragraph should not be hyphenated.
- When the last line of a page continues on the next spread (if the reader has to turn the page) the last word of that line should not be hyphenated.
- Display type should not be hyphenated.
- Proper names should not be hyphenated.

In addition, if possible (or practical):

- Avoid a hyphenated line at the top of a page or text column.
- Avoid a hyphenated line at the bottom of a page or text column.

Here are some other guidelines for breaking lines (without hyphens) :

- Avoid breaking a line before an em dash.
- Never break a line at an en dash.
- Don't break long numbers, such as $1,656,000.
- Avoid hyphenation that might trip the reader, such as *read-just* for *re-adjust*.
- Don't let a line break in the middle of an ellipsis (. . .).
- Don't let an ellipsis appear alone as the last line of a paragraph.
- Don't allow hyphenation in extracts or centered text.

Aesthetic Rags

In text set with ragged margins, the degree of raggedness can be described on a scale of *tight* to *wild*. In a tight rag, the variations between line lengths are very small. If a rag is set too tight, it can look like badly justified type, with the effect of looking sloppy rather than neat.

In a wild rag, the variations in line length are more extreme. Ragged copy set without hyphenation will tend to be wild. It's more difficult to create a good looking wild rag because, for example, a series of consecutive short or long lines can create distracting shapes in the margin.

When setting type with ragged margins, keep the quality of the rag consistent throughout the document. Some composition programs let you specify how the rag should develop. One method enables you to define a zone a small distance from the margin in which no two consecutive lines will be allowed to end. This assures that successive lines will establish a long-short-long pattern that will prevent the margin from assuming shapes or having one paragraph setting on an apparently wider or shorter measure than others.

Here are some specific rules about setting with ragged margins:

- Create paragraph shapes that are essentially rectangular, without exaggerated concave or convex margins.
- Avoid single long lines that appear to exceed the measure.
- Avoid a short line at the start of a page or column.
- Avoid having a short line/long line sequence at the end of a paragraph.
- Avoid a long line before a short last line of a paragraph.

Lines of display type must always be broken with the sense of the text in mind. The rhythm of the text takes precedence over the shape of the rag:

Volunteers from
Mars Candy Company
Organize Program
for Handicapped

not:

Volunteers from Mars
Candy Company Organize
Program for Handicapped

To correct minor problems with rags, use your program's *line-ending command*. This acts like a carriage return but doesn't signal the start of a new paragraph. In computer typography, this is called *hard-ending* the lines (see Figure 1.4).

If there are a lot of bad rags in your text, the problem may be with the point size and line length you've specified, and that your program is having a hard time justifying the text. Problem rags may also develop in narrow margins with programs that use logic-based

(a)

Those, then, who controvert the principle that the Constitution is to be considered, in court, as a paramount law are reduced to the necessity of maintaining that courts must close their eyes on the Constitution and see only the law. This doctrine would subvert the very foundation of all written constitutions.

(b)

Those, then, who controvert the principle that the Constitution is to be considered, in court, as a paramount law are reduced to the necessity of maintaining that courts must close their eyes on the Constitution and see only the law. This doctrine would subvert the very foundation of all written constitutions.

(c)

Recognition of the falsity of material wealth as the standard of success goes hand in hand with the abandonment of the false belief that public office and high political position are to be valued only by the standards of pride and place and personal profit; and there must be an end to a conduct in banking and in business which too often has given to a sacred trust the likeness of callous and selfish wrongdoing.

(d)

Recognition of the falsity of material wealth as the standard of success goes hand in hand with the abandonment of the false belief that public office and high political position are to be valued only by the standards of pride and place and personal profit; and there must be an end to a conduct in banking and in business which too often has given to a sacred trust the likeness of callous and selfish wrongdoing.

Figure 1.4

To create attractive and unobtrusive ragged margins, some tidying up by hand is often needed. The rag in paragraph (a) has three long lines protruding beyond short ones in between. Breaking the first line, using a soft carriage return, causes the rest of the lines to rebreak, giving paragraph (b) a more natural shape. Even though the first line now falls well short of the margin, it's hardly noticeable, and the overall effect is much improved.

In the second pair, paragraph (c) has a potbellied margin that stands out oddly on the page. Tightening the tracking of the first line brings part of a word up from the second line, and the paragraph is restored to a more rectangular shape in example (d).

hyphenation; these programs tend to hyphenate less than dictionary-based programs. If your program allows it, set the program to hyphenate more liberally. Finally, you may opt to allow your program to set more consecutive hyphenated lines, which will also help smooth the rag.

Rags in Centered Text

In centered text, the main thing to avoid is a shape that's too rectangular.

In a centered text block of two lines, the first line should be longer than the second, but much less than twice as long. It's better to have both lines set short of the measure than have one line too much longer than the other.

In centered text of three lines or more, avoid pyramid and inverted pyramid shapes. Convex margins (where lines start short, get longer, then get shorter again) can look good if the curve is not too perfect. But a ragged margin within a generally curving margin is best.

If centered lines follow a long-short-long-short pattern, don't let the first or last lines be much longer than those that follow or precede them.

Don't hyphenate centered lines, even at hard hyphens.

Widows and Orphans

Definitions of these terms vary somewhat. In type composition programs, a *widow* is a very short last line of a paragraph. Widows are also the first line or two of a paragraph when they occur as the last line or lines in a page or column. An *orphan* is the last line or two of a paragraph that appear at the top of a page or column. Both are undesirable because they fracture the neat rectangle that the text forms on the page.

Ideally, the last lines of paragraphs should ideally fill at least 20 percent of the measure, but this is often impractical. At the very least, a last line should be long enough to extend well past the paragraph indent in the line below it. *Hyphenated widows*—where the widow is composed of a word fragment—should not be allowed.

No paragraph should begin less than three lines from the bottom of a page.

No column or page should begin with a paragraph fragment of less than two full lines or less than three lines if the last line is short.

Subheadings should not fall within three lines of the bottom of a page or column. And when possible, also avoid having them appear as the top line of a page or column.

Sometimes a minor tracking change can eliminate a last-line widow or cause the text to rerag, thereby eliminating orphans or paragraph widows. Such tracking changes must be very subtle to avoid changing the color of the lines or paragraphs affected.

Often, widow and orphan problems are best resolved editorially. Reducing or adding text can eliminate short lines or paragraphs.

Widows and orphans can also be resolved through *vertical justification*. This is a capability of some composition programs that makes minor adjustments to the leading of a column or page to correct vertical spacing problems. It can be used to pull orphans back onto previous pages or push text forward to lengthen them. It can also be used to control the location of subheadings too close to the tops or bottoms of pages. However, vertical justification changes must be kept very subtle to avoid changing the type color of the column or page. It's generally more useful on one-column pages, where the binding gutter (the inner page margin) obscures any variation in leading between the two facing pages.

When repairing widows and orphans, pay attention to the ripple effect you create; fixing a problem on one page can create more problems on the following pages.

Loose and Tight Lines

Your program may not always be able to compose all lines of text with the same apparent spacing. Some lines can appear too tight and others too loose. The problem may have several sources. First, the values that have been specified for word and letter spacing may be too liberal, thus allowing the software too much leeway in fitting the lines. Second, the measure may be too narrow for the point size specified. This forces the program to awkward extremes in order to fit the lines. Third, single lines may have problems because the program has been restrained from hyphenating. This can happen when the last word of a line is long and cannot be hyphenated, is unfamiliar to the program's dictionary, or can't be algorithmically hyphenated, or because the limit for consecutive hyphenated lines has been reached.

Composition programs will typically highlight loose or tight lines, but most word processing programs will not. In any case, these problem lines should be sought out during proofreading.

Individual loose and tight lines can be fixed in one of three ways:

- By manually hyphenating the problem line using a soft hyphen.
- By adjusting the tracking of the line or paragraph—such tracking changes must be very subtle.
- By making a copy change that will cause the line or paragraph to recompose.

Never alter character widths to fix loose or tight lines.

Typographic Manuscript Conventions

The characters you can produce with a typewriter are a subset of the fuller family of characters used in professional typesetting (see Chapter 3). In addition, typesetting uses some spacing conventions differently from those you may be used to from typewriting or word processing. The following is a summary of the differences you'll encounter most often.

Spaces

In typeset pages, never use multiple word spaces. Unlike typewritten text, only one word space should follow the period at the end of a sentence. And multiple word spaces shouldn't be used to create paragraph indents. This is because typesetting programs routinely stretch and squeeze word spaces to fit the type into the specified *measure*, or line length. This stretching and squeezing could cause the width of your indents to vary from paragraph to paragraph (see *Indents* below).

To create spaces wider than a word space, use *fixed spaces: em, en, thin* and *figure spaces*. They're called fixed spaces because, unlike word spaces, they are not stretched or squeezed during text composition. Not all word processors offer these spaces, but they are standard in page makeup programs. They can be used singly or in multiples and combinations.

The width of an em space is equal to the point size of the type you've specified. Therefore, an em space in 14-point type is 14 points wide; an em space in 24-point type is 24 points wide. An en space is equal to half the width of an em space, and a thin space (which most page makeup programs let you define yourself) is typically equal to about half an en or one-quarter of an em. A figure space is the same width as a numeral and is used for aligning numbers in tabular matter.

Indents

Indents, such as those used for paragraphs, are best created with your program's indent commands. In menu-driven programs indents are typically defined in the paragraph menu. Using the Tab key to create paragraph indents should be avoided for two reasons. First, it's easier to change the depth of a paragraph indent by using a paragraph indent command than it is to redefine the width of the tab. This also lets you save your tab definitions for use in a tabular matter in the same document. Also, you can make global indent changes without affecting your tabbed material.

Second, tab locations are defined in terms of their positions on the page; they are not defined relative to the position of the text in which they occur. For example, say you have a column of type with a half-inch paragraph indent that you created by hitting the Tab key. If you later decide to indent that entire column of type, you'll find that your paragraph indents have become shallower—the left margin of the text column may have moved to the right, but the starting points of the tabbed lines remain unchanged. This is because the tab-set indent is keyed to a position on the page. It's locked in place, instead of being keyed to the left edge of the other lines in the paragraph, as a paragraph indent should be.

A paragraph indent created with an indent command is defined in relation to where the lines of text actually begin. If you indent that text to the right, the first-line paragraph indent will slide over also, maintaining its proper depth relative to the block of text.

Line Endings

In general, word processors and typesetting programs automatically break lines within a paragraph. They do it whenever a line has filled the measure. In these programs, hitting the Return key immediately ends a line and signals the start of a new paragraph. A carriage return can also automatically trigger certain typographical effects, such as the indention of the line immediately following it, which creates a first-line paragraph indent.

However, you may want to manually end a line without ending the paragraph. To do this, most programs also offer a soft carriage return, or line ending command. This command breaks the line and starts a new one without creating a new paragraph. This is an easy way to create an unindented list when a normal carriage return would trigger a paragraph indent.

Whenever practical, you should avoid using multiple carriage returns to create vertical space on a page. Generally, the places where you'd like to add space are above or below a particular text element, such as a subheading. In these cases, use your program's style sheet to add the extra space into the typographic description of that text element (see Tags, Style Sheets, and Generic Markup in this chapter for details). This enables you to change your mind about the depth of any added space and easily reformat it throughout the document. All you have to do is redefine how much space should precede that subheading, and the spacing will be globally corrected automatically.

However, there are exceptions to this "ban" on multiple carriage returns. They occur in ASCII files, where multiple carriage returns are the only way to create extra vertical space on the page, and in multiple-column pages in which you want all text lines across the page to align on the same baselines. Such an alignment is common in newsletters and magazines. The only way to ensure this alignment is to add extra space between lines in the columns only in full line-space increments. This is easily created by hitting the Return key. For more on line spacing and text alignment, see Mechanical Alignment in Chapter 2.

Hyphens and Dashes

The hyphen is the shortest of three typographic dashes, and the only one available on the typewriter and many word processors. It's also the only one that's an ASCII character. The other two are the *em dash* (one em in width) and the *en dash* (one en wide).

There are two kinds of hyphens: hard hyphens are used to link compound words, and you type them yourself into a manuscript; soft hyphens are added to a manuscript by your computer program. Soft hyphens link the parts of a word has been broken at the end of a line. Don't add hard hyphens at the end of a line. If you have to hyphenate a line-ending word manually, use your program's *soft* or *discretionary hyphen*, not the hyphen you see printed on your keyboard. Your program's manual will tell you how to use discretionary hyphens (the procedure varies slightly from program to program). A discretionary hyphen will only appear when a word has to be broken in order to fit a line of type. If a word containing a discretionary hyphen occurs in the middle of a line, the hyphen will not appear.

By contrast, a *hard hyphen* is the one you get by hitting the hyphen key. This is a standard ASCII keystroke and a permanent addition to your manuscript. It is used to connect the parts of a compound word. If in later editing that word moves into the middle of a line, the hyphen will move with it. Therefore, use hard hyphens only when you want them to be permanent fixtures in your manuscript, as when creating compound words such as *ping-pong*.

Don't make a dash with two hyphens, unless you're creating an ASCII file in which the double hyphens will later be replaced by dashes. For more on the proper use of hyphens and dashes, see the first two sections in Chapter 3.

Quotation Marks

Typeset quotation marks and apostrophes (" ' ' ") are different from the typewriter-style quotation marks found on your keyboard (" '). The typewriter-style quotes, though, are ASCII characters, while their typographic counterparts are not. Don't use the typewriter-style quotes except when creating ASCII documents. For how to handle typewriter-style quotes in ASCII documents so they can be converted into opening and closing quotation marks, see Search and Replace Formatting Strategies for Tagged ASCII Manuscripts in Chapter 6.

When italicized, typewriter-style quotes are useful for creating the single and double *primes* (' ") that indicate feet, inches, minutes, and seconds. But remember that the italicization will not be preserved when the file is saved in ASCII format.

Pi Characters

Pi characters are non-ASCII utility characters often used to highlight listed items, to indicate footnotes, and to draw attention to particular passages of text. For a full discussion of these characters, see Spacing of Symbols and Common Pi Characters in Chapter 3.

Typographic Style

A lot of what passes for good design is no more than sound, traditional typographic practice. If you follow the rules and guidelines in this chapter, many documents will virtually design themselves.

Margin Styles

Lines of text and paragraphs that completely fill their specified measures are called *justified*. Lines that fall short of their specified measures are called *ragged*. Justified margins are generally straight and vertical, as in most book and newspaper text. Ragged margins are found most often in magazines, newsletters, and reports.

A ragged margin is formed by a text composition program when no effort is made to stretch or squeeze the line to fill the measure. In these cases, as on a typewriter, the extra space is left along one margin. When this extra space is left along the righthand margin, you get *flush-left/ragged-right* copy. When it's left along the left-hand margin, you get *flush-right/ragged-left* copy. When the extra space is divided equally at both ends of the line, you get *centered* copy. Centered copy is occasionally called *ragged center*, even though this makes no syntactical sense.

Justified margins are typically straight and parallel. But the margins of justified lines need not be parallel, vertical, or even straight. A block of type may have oblique sides (called *skewed* margins) or it may be in the shape of a circle or other curve. As long as the lines of type fill each specified measure fully from margin to margin, the lines are said to be justified.

Ragged Margins

Ragged margins create more of an informal effect than justified margins. They also work better in multicolumn pages, so they're rarely seen in books, except in front and back matter such as prefaces, forewords, and colophons. In a multicolumn page, such as in a newsletter, ragged margins loosen the layout and keep pages from looking too stiff. In sparsely illustrated pages, they also add additional white space and graphic interest to the page.

Avoid wild rags (see Aesthetic Rags in Chapter 1) in narrow columns. If a rag is too jagged, the column loses its rectangular identity and page geometry becomes sloppy. In addition, wild rags in narrow columns make reading difficult because the reader can't establish a rhythm due to the zigzagging between the long and short lines. The shortest line in a ragged column should be no less than 75 percent of the length of the longest line.

Multicolumn texts set with ragged margins can be set with narrower gutters between columns than justified text. Visually, the white space of the ragged margin merges with the gutter, making it look wider. The wilder the rag, the narrower the gutter can be. On a typical 8½-by-11-inch three-column newsletter page, an 18-point gutter would be considered normal for justified text, but this space can be reduced to 12 points or less for columns set ragged-right.

Avoid flush-right, ragged-left copy except in very short passages, such as in captions or call-outs. A flush left margin makes it easier for the eye to settle on the correct lines during reading. Ragged-left margins make for slow going.

Don't allow hyphenation in centered text.

Don't use first-line indents in centered text or ragged-left text.

Justified Margins

Avoid justified copy set in narrow columns. When the width of your measure (in picas) approaches the size of your type (in points) justified margins can create bad word and letter spacing. For example, 11-point type over a 13-pica measure is best set ragged-right. Newspapers illustrate this, where word and letter spacing is often grossly exaggerated to justify type across narrow columns.

Justified type on multicolumn pages does not need gutter rules to separate the columns: the straight, justified margins are sufficient to delineate the space on the page. If a design calls for gutter rules, the gutter should be widened by 4 points or so to keep the text columns from looking too crowded.

Inserting some ragged copy on an otherwise justified page can break up the blockiness to which all-justified pages are prone.

Skews and Wraps

Margins that are not vertical or whose shapes are not straight are called shaped margins. They consist of *skews* (straight nonvertical margins) and *wraps* (text margins fitted around a graphic or another piece of text). Both skews and wraps are most commonly used in advertising, where readability takes a back-seat to their eye-catching appeal. With the advent of desktop publishing, wraps and skews have also become popular in newsletters and magazines, because the technology makes them easy to create.

Skews and wraps typically narrow the measure at which text is set, which often creates composition problems. Avoid wraps and skews that further constrict already narrow measures. If a design calls for a margin to be narrowed by a skew or wrap, pay close attention to word and letter spacing in the narrowed area. Also, make spacing, tracking, hyphenation, and copy adjustments as necessary to help the type to compose well.

Skewed margins are most effective when used with justified margins, which highlight the geometry of the skew. A skew in ragged copy can look crooked and wobbly instead of crisp and angular.

Wraps around smooth geometric shapes also look best in justified copy, because the line endings more closely mirror the shape being wrapped.

When creating rectangular wraps, such as for inset photographs, make sure the type color in the area of constricted measure matches that of the surrounding text. In narrower columns, the text will tend to set much more loosely.

Do not set a rectangular wrap that straddles two ragged-margin columns, such as in the middle of a two-column page. In such a case, the right-hand side of the open rectangle will have a flush margin, and the left-hand side will have an awkwardly contrasting ragged margin.

When a wrap or skew occurs on the left-hand margin, you may have to deepen first-line indents so they'll remain visible.

Indention Style

Indention is any variation in measure. A series of indented lines constitutes a *running indent*. When the depth of the indent varies from line to line, the result is a wrap or skew (see above).

The other basic kinds of indents are *first-line indent, hanging indent,* and *indent on text.*

Running Indents

A running indent moves the margin or margins closer to the center of the text column for a number of lines. Left indents and right indents are two kinds of running indents. Because other indents, such as the first-line indent, are based on this margin, they are preserved when a running indent is added to the text. For example, when a 15-pica-wide column with a one-em paragraph indent is set with a 2-pica left indent, it becomes a 13-pica-wide column, but it retains the one-em indent on the first line.

First-Line Indent

A *first-line indent* is often called a *paragraph indent.* It can be pro-grammed to automatically appear on the next line following a paragraph-ending command. This is typically a Return (or carriage return) in most desktop publishing programs.

Paragraph indents should not be created with the Tab key. If paragraph indents are created with an indent command, they can be altered much more easily. Leave tabs for tabular matter.

First line indents are generally specified in ems and ens, but most word processors and desktop publishing programs would have you translate that into points or picas and points.

A first-line indent visually punctuates the page for the benefit of the reader. It reflects both page and text structure. The wider the measure, the deeper a first-line indent can be. In fact, a deep first-line indent helps break up the gray of all-text pages and makes large pages of text seem less imposing. Because paragraph indents provide a breather for the reader, a deeper indent gives the reader a chance for a deeper breath.

Depths of first-line indents vary widely in books and magazines. As a general rule, well-proportioned first line indents range from 7 to 10 percent of the measure. This means that a typical 3-column newsletter would have em or em-en indents. Two ems are about the maximum. As columns get wider, though, paragraph indents do not grow at as rapid a pace. At a 30-pica measure, a 4-em indent would be acceptable, but unusually wide.

Hanging Indent

In a hanging indent, the first line of the paragraph extends to the full measure, and the lines that follow are indented from the left. This is common in indexes, catalogs, and directories.

Don't use a hanging indent in conjunction with a first-line indent, because they cancel each other out.

Hanging indents should be kept fairly shallow. What they may lack in depth they make up for in duration, making them graphically quite strong.

Avoid hanging indents in very narrow columns. Further constricting the measure may cause composition problems.

A variation of the hanging indent extends the first line or lines of the paragraph to extend out to the left, beyond the margin of the rest of the text, while the rest of the paragraph maintains its normal measure. This configuration is called, oddly, an *outdent*.

Indent on Text

Although you specify the depth of most indents in picas and points, the depth of an indent on text is determined by the width of a passage of typeset matter, whose exact width in picas and points can't be known without printing a sample first to measure it. An indent on text is a kind of hanging indent.

Indents on text are useful for creating lists with "hanging" bullets (where the text is indented a distance equivalent to the width of the bullet and the word space that follows it) and in catalog work (where a product description following a product name must be indented by the width of that name).

To set an indent on text, you set the type that determines the depth of the indent and then mark the position with a special keystroke. Succeeding lines in that paragraph will align flush left at the point of this marker, creating a hanging indent. The indent is usually automatically cancelled when an end-of-paragraph command (usually a Return) is invoked.

Drop Caps and Standing Caps

Oversized initial capitals are often used to highlight the beginning of a chapter or text section. They are also used in place of subheads to denote a transition in the text. Oversized capitals used in this role must make editorial sense—they must only be placed where there is a break in the sense or flow of the text. They should not be used simply for their design effect on the page.

When an oversized initial cap extends below the first line of paragraph text, it's called a *drop cap*. When it stands on the first baseline of the paragraph it's called a *standing cap*.

Drop Caps

A drop cap should always align on one of the baselines of the paragraph text (see Figure 2.1). Similarly, it should top-align with or

Among the numerous advantages promised by a well constructed Union, none deserves to be more accurately developed than its tendency to break and control the violence of faction.

When a drop-cap letter's shape leans away from the paragraph, it seems to lose its role as part of the text. In the upper sample here, the *A* is off on its own, and the paragraph seems to begin with *mong*. Shaping the text around the letter helps the two read as one.

Among the numerous advantages promised by a well constructed Union, none deserves to be more accurately developed than its tendency to break and control the violence of faction.

The Sun never shined on a cause of greater worth. 'Tis not the affair of a City, a County, a Province, or a Kingdom; but of a Continent—of at least one-eighth part of the habitable Globe.

Letters that reach out to the text make the best drop caps. Here, the *T* clearly reads with the paragraph. The small-caps text shown here is a common device used with drop caps to enhance the relationship between capital and text.

In contemplating the causes which disturb our union, it occurs as a matter of serious concern, that any ground should have been furnished for characterizing parties by geographical discriminations: Northern and Southern; Atlantic and Western . . . .

Sans serif faces are often used for drop caps because their clean geometric shapes make them strong graphic players on the page. Sometimes, though, they can be too graphic and not literal enough, as in the case of this *I*, which hardly looks like a letter at all.

On the occasion corresponding to this four years ago, all thoughts were anxiously directed to an impending civil war. All dreaded it—all sought to avert it.

The positioning of drop caps often has to be adjusted by hand. Here, in order to get it to look properly aligned, the *O* has been pushed to the left to extend out beyond the margin and below the baseline of the third line of type.

Figure 2.1

rise slightly above the ascender line of the first line of the paragraph. Take care when using a *J* as a drop cap, because in most text faces this character extends below the baseline. This means that in a manuscript where all other drop caps are four lines deep, the indent for a *J* may have to be five or six lines deep. To preserve a consistent appearance to your drops caps, consider avoiding using a J as a drop cap in those faces where it doesn't base-align. The *Q* may present a similar problem.

Drop caps should be a minimum of three lines deep; two-line drop caps are graphically weak, except in very narrow columns. In multicolumn pages with three or more columns, if a drop cap is more than five lines deep, consider condensing the width of the drop cap to keep its width in balance with the width of the text column. In one- and two-column pages, this limit can safely be extended to seven or eight lines.

Drop caps need not be in the same typeface as the rest of the paragraph. Sans serif characters are often used as drop caps because their clean geometry works well with a simple rectangular indent.

Avoid using extended or expanded characters as drop caps.

Several drop caps can appear on a single multicolumn page, but on single-column pages avoid having more than one drop cap per page.

Paragraphs with drop caps should be separated from the preceding paragraphs by extra leading, typically a line space. Larger drop caps need more additional lead.

Drop caps must be set so that their role in the text is clear. If the drop cap is too far from the text or is overdesigned (extremely condensed or in a wildly contrasting typeface) the reader may see it as a graphic element rather than as part of the text. For this reason, letters such as *L* don't make good drop caps—their shapes distance them from the text they are a part of. For these letters, simple rectangular indents in the paragraph may not suffice, and shaped indents are often used (see Figure 2.1).

Shaped indents around drop caps must provide sufficient space to keep the text from smothering the drop cap. In general, it's better to have only the first line of the paragraph reach toward the drop cap, and leave the following lines on a consistent indent.

Because of their size, drop caps may not appear to align flush left with the rest of the paragraph. This is because every character is set with a small amount of white space on either side that keeps it from touching adjoining letters. These spaces are called the *side bearings* of the characters. When you enlarge a character such as a drop cap, you also enlarge its side bearings. This can make a large drop cap appear to be indented slightly from the margin. In addition, some characters need to extend slightly outside of the margin in order to appear properly aligned. For more on this subject, see the section called Mechanical Alignment in this chapter.

Standing Caps

Standing caps cannot be as large as drop caps because they create too wide a gap between paragraphs and because large standing caps can easily loose contact with the text they begin. Standing caps can be as small as twice the size of the paragraph text, and unlike drop caps, they can be set at any increment larger than that.

In general, standing caps look best when set in the same typeface as the text.

Standing caps can be used with first-line indents and are often used with quite extreme indents, but only in opening paragraphs.

Standing caps can be set in expanded characters because their link to the text is more obvious and direct. Also, unlike drop caps, the extra white space they create on the page rests above the paragraph, not within it, so their connection to the paragraph is clearer.

Index Style

Indexes are typically set in a multicolumn format, using hanging indents (see Indention Style in this chapter) with ragged right margins. They are also set in a smaller point size than the main text.

Indexes can be set in the indented or run-in style. In the former, each index subentry starts on its own indented line. In the latter, all subentries are run in with the main entry heading, separated by semicolons. Indexes set in run-in style take up less space than indented indexes. In each, the page number is separated from the entry or subentry by a comma.

An index typically starts on a right-hand, *recto* page.

On an 8½-by-11-inch page, a three-column index works best.

Page references to pictures, photos, or other illustrations are typically highlighted by using italic or boldface.

If an index page begins midentry, use a *jump line* to alert readers to their position in the index:

Consumer Fraud (continued)

A line space is sufficient to create alphabetical divisions in an index, such as separating the *A*'s from the *B*'s.

Indented-Style Indexes

Indented-style indexes are easier for the reader to use, especially if the index is complex.

In an indented-style index, each main entry sets flush left. Runovers (continuations of the first line, also called *turnovers* or *turnlines*) are indented, typically two ems. Subentries are indented, usually by one em, and their runovers are also indented two ems. If sub-subentries exist, you may have to adjust the indention scheme of the index to prevent these lines and their runovers from becoming too short.

A typical indented-style index entry might be as follows:

Consumer fraud
    criminal penalties for, 124
    hot lines, popularity of, 177
    increase in 1980s, 187–210
    mail fraud, 191
    recidivism rates, 251
    telephone fraud, 205

Run-in–Style Indexes

In indexes set in the run-in style, the main entry sets flush left, and all sub-entries run in directly behind it. All runovers are indented, typically one em. There is only one level of indent in a run-in index.

A typical run-in index entry might be as follows:

Consumer fraud
    criminal penalties for, 124;
    hot lines, popularity of,
    177; increase in 1980s,
    187–210; recidivism
    rates, 251

Footnote Style

Footnotes can be set at the bottoms of the pages on which they are cited, at the end of the chapter, or at the end of the document. Grouping footnotes together and numbering them makes page composition much easier, but it's impractical for documents with only occasional unnumbered footnotes.

Where footnotes are used occasionally and are unnumbered, they're flagged in text with common typographical symbols, such as asterisks and daggers. If more than one such footnote occurs on a page, these symbols are used in a standard order:

    * asterisk, for first footnote on the page
    † dagger, for the second
    ‡ double dagger, for the third

If more than three footnotes appear on a page, you should use numbers. The numbers should be set as superior or superscript figures in a point size 60 to 70 percent of the size of the surrounding text.

In the footnote, the number should be followed by a word space that is set in the size of the footnote text, not in the size of the superior.

Footnote copy should be set smaller than the body text, preferably two or three point sizes smaller.

The typographic format of a footnote is more a design issue than a typographic one. Footnotes that appear at the bottom of the page are generally given a line space between the end of the text and the footnote. In multicolumn pages, the last line of the footnote should be set on the same baseline as the last line of the longest text columns on other pages. In single-column pages, it should base-align with the last line of text on the facing page.

In multicolumn pages, unless it is very lengthy, set the footnote in the same column and measure in which it was cited. The leading of the footnote should be appropriate to the point size in which it is set. It does not have to match the leading of the body text.

When footnotes are grouped at the end of a chapter or document, they are typically either indented in the manner of the body text or set flush left and separated by extra leading, typically half-line spaces.

Page Numbering

Printed pages are divided into *recto* (right-hand) and *verso* (left-hand). In a document whose pages are printed only on one side (as are most word-processed documents) all pages are called recto pages. In two-sided documents, recto pages get odd-numbered *folios* (page numbers), and verso pages get even numbers.

There is no typographic standard for the position or format of folios. These decisions are typically the prerogative of the designer. However, some placements and treatments are fairly standard.

Folios are commonly placed flush against the outer margins of the text, odd numbers on the right margin, even numbers on the left margin. Folios aligned in this way may be set above or below the text block. A standard position for such folios is with one line space of white space between the folio and the text block.

When the page has a running head or running foot and the folio appears in the same part of the page, the folio is set on the same baseline as the running copy. The running copy may be centered, set flush against the inside text margin of the page, or separated from the folio by a fixed space.

Folios are also commonly centered on the page, again either above or below the text block with an intervening line space.

Folios are also commonly set in the same typeface, size, and weight as the text copy.

Rules, Boxes, and Underscores

Typographic lines are called *rules*. They are defined by their thickness, which is expressed in points. The exception is the *hairline*, which is defined differently by various composition programs, though it is typically ⅛ point or less. A double rule made up of rules of differing weights is called a *compound rule* or *Scotch rule*. A dashed or dotted rule is called a *coupon rule*.

Composition programs may set rules as an integral part of the text or as an independent graphic entity. In either case, it's best to think of rules as having their own baselines on which they sit. This enables you to specify base-to-base measurements consistently for both type and rules on a page. For instance, a rule across the top of a page should sit on a specific grid line, and the top line of type on the same page should sit on a baseline at a prescribed distance below that.

Avoid using the underscore character to build rules. This character's weight varies with the point size it's set in, and you'll never get it to match other rules of specific weight. Nevertheless, the underscore character may be useful for creating the "blanks" in simple forms and coupons created with a word processor.

Always use your program's "snap-to" feature or other grid-alignment tool to make sure rules align precisely and abut each other cleanly.

When creating a box that will be filled with photomechanical artwork, such as a halftone photograph or piece of four-color art, the rules that comprise the box should be at least a half-point thick. This allows some leeway in positioning the graphic work within the box. If hairline rules are used, it's almost impossible to align the graphic or photo precisely within it, and some of the image may extend slightly outside of the box. If all artwork is being placed on the page using the computer, this is not a problem.

Underscores beneath type have no distinct typographic role except as a form of graphic emphasis. Generally, underscores created on a typewriter are converted into italics in typeset matter. To use typographic underscores effectively, your composition program should give you control over the thickness of the underscore and how far it sets below the baseline. It must also be able to turn the underscore off automatically under characters with descenders, otherwise the underscore will cross over them. If your program can't accommodate descenders in this way, you should only use underscores with all-caps or material set in caps and small caps.

As an alternative, you can manually set underscores by setting rules at a precise distance below the text baseline. This is tedious, though, and unless your program enables you to link the rules to the text, they'll fall out of alignment if the position of the text is altered.

In setting underscores, the weight of the rule should be less than the average stroke weight of the text being underscored.

Leaders

A *leader* is a series of characters—usually periods—that links separate but related pieces of text across a page or column. For example, prices on a menu are commonly separated by leaders from the names of the dishes. Leader dots are traditional, as well, in tables of contents and catalog work.

Unless the distance between the text elements is large, such as on a typical menu, leaders tend to clutter more than clarify. If lines are so tightly spaced that the reader's eye has trouble scanning accurately from left to right, leader dots probably won't improve matters. Instead, the reader's eye will wander into a field of dots where it's just as likely to get lost. If the lines are spaced far enough apart to make the leader lines easy to follow, they probably aren't necessary in the first place.

Always let your program create leaders for you: don't assemble them one dot at a time. Composition programs typically create leaders as tab fills. To use these, specify a "fill" character when defining your tab fields. As you move from tab to tab with the Tab key, the "fill" character will automatically produce a leader. Some code-driven composition programs simply offer a character-fill command that does the same job without having to define any tabs. The leader that's created simply pushes the surrounding text out to the margins. In either case, computer-generated leaders automatically align the leader dots into vertical rows.

Screens

Screens have become a typographical concern since desktop publishing technology added them to type composition programs. Screens are arrays of tiny dots that create the effect of a shade of gray or a color tint. They are commonly used to highlight boxed areas of a page, such as a sidebar, that stand apart from the main text. Screens are specified as a percentage of total ink coverage, with a solid color equalling 100 percent. In a 10 percent screen, then, the dots cover 10 percent of the area being screened.

Type set on desktop laser printers should not be set over screens except in display sizes because the screens these printers create is too coarse, making the text hard to read. As desktop laser printers improve, and the screen dots they can create become finer, this will be less of a problem.

In type set on a high-resolution phototypesetter or *imagesetter* (a phototypesetter capable of printing graphic images as well as type), avoid setting type over a gray screen of more than 20 percent. At this point, the reduced contrast between the type and its background begins to affect legibility. When screens are printed in colors, especially light colors, this problem is reduced. It's best to consult a commercial printer before setting type over more heavily screened colors.

Mechanical Alignment

Precise alignment of text and graphic elements gives order and harmony to a page, making it more inviting for the reader and easier to read. In general, every page element needs a reason to be where it is. A design grid grid should accommodate the placement of virtually all page elements and simplify most alignment decisions (see The Page Grid in this chapter). But there are also many other small- and large-scale alignment issues to tend to. The following is a list of the various type alignments and where and how to use them.

Top Alignment

Top-aligned elements use the type's ascent line as a point of alignment. At the top of a three-column newsletter page, for instance, a boxed photograph may top align with the top line of a column of text on the same page. In this case, the top edge of the box aligns with the ascent line of the first line of text.

Top-alignment occurs more often at the character level. In advertising copy, dollar and cents signs are often set in small point sizes and top-aligned with the price numbers (see Figure 2.2). Characters that typically top-align include the copyright mark (©), the trademark symbol (™), the registered trademark symbol (®), and the signature mark symbol (SM). The numerators of fractions also top-align (see Numerals, Numbers, Dates, and Fractions in Chapter 4).

Figure 2.2
In the top sample, the cent sign has been set at half its normal size and raised up to top-align with the numerals to its left. The bullet is centered on cap height.

In the bottom sample, the bullet has been lowered to center on x-height, to align it more logically with the lowercase initial *n*.

Not all of these characters will automatically top-align. For example, the copyright symbol, used in such lines as "© Boston University, 1991," exists in most fonts as a cap-height character. To top-align such characters, set them as superiors or superscripts, changing their size and leading as necessary in your program to move them into position. As top-aligned superiors, their size should be about two-thirds that of the surrounding text. In display sizes, they should set even smaller, down to one-third or less of the size of the surrounding type.

Base Alignment

This is the most common form of text alignment, and most text base-aligns automatically. Certain utility characters, also called *pi characters* (see Chapter 3), are best used when base-aligned. The most common of these is the *ballot box* (□), popular for coupons and forms.

The bottoms of illustration boxes in multicolumn pages should also base align with the text in adjoining columns. Likewise, captions in such pages look more precisely positioned when their first lines are base-aligned with text in adjoining columns.

In multicolumn pages such as in newsletters, pages look better organized when the lines of the running text (that is, not sidebar or boxed text) in all the columns fall on common baselines. A ruler held along the baseline of a line in one column would also line up with the baselines of lines in the other columns. To facilitate this alignment, keep the leading consistent throughout all the columns, and add space (such as around subheads) only in whole-line increments.

At a minimum, the top line of text on every page should align on the same grid line, and all of the bottom lines in all of the columns should base-align.

To assist in this, some programs offer *vertical justification,* which minutely adjusts the leading throughout a column or page. This will assure that the baselines of the last lines on all pages will fall on the same grid line. Vertical justification can also be used to solve layout dilemmas, such as widows, orphans, and subheads that appear at the tops or bottoms of columns (see Widows and Orphans in Chapter 1).

Centering on Cap Height, X-Height

Centering on cap height assumes that an imaginary horizontal line passes midway through the height of the capital letters; that is, half way between the capital line and the base line. Some pi characters, notably *bullets* (•) should center on cap height. Likewise, any pi character used to highlight items in a list—such as diamonds (♦), and arrows (⇨)—should center on cap height.

The exception is when using such characters in front of lower-case letters, as in Figure 2.2. In these cases, the pi characters should center on x-height to look properly aligned.

Mechanical Centering

When you manually break lines of centered text to achieve a good rag, take care to break the lines after word spaces and not before them. When fitting lines, composition programs ignore word spaces at the ends of lines. But most word processors and desktop publishing programs will include spaces that appear at the beginning of lines. When you break centered lines and cause them to begin with a word space, those lines will appear off-center to the right. (See Horizontal Optical Centering below.)

Optical Alignment

Computer programs align type elements with great mathematical precision. Sometimes, though, type that is mechanically aligned doesn't *look* aligned.

Horizontal Optical Centering

Lines of centered text are prone to look off-center because characters that begin or end them can vary in their graphic strength. As with a word space that begins a line (see Mechanical Centering above), a weak character, such as a punctuation mark (especially double quotation marks) will make a line seem off-center. Likewise, a graphically strong character at the beginning or end of a line, such as a wide capital letter, can also seem to pull a line off-center. A line that begins or ends with a series of small words can have the same effect, because the several word spaces that appear between them tend to unbalance the line (see Figure 2.3).

A centered heading over a column of flush-left/ragged-right text will look off-center to the right because the heading is centered over the white space in the ragged margin as well as the column text itself. A handy rule of thumb for correcting this is to measure the difference between shortest and longest lines in the ragged text, divide this amount by three, and indent the centered head to the left by the quotient. This will generally restore optical centering.

In tables, wide headings centered over narrow flush-left or flush-right columns can look wildly misaligned. To avoid this, make tab columns as narrow as possible. In tables with flush-right copy, such as in financial tables, tab settings for headings may have to be different from the tabs settings of the numbers below them to get the alignment to look right. For more details on tabular alignment, see Chapter 5.

"When they say go," said
Dr. King, "I go...."

"When they say go," said
Dr. King, "I go...."

Figure 2.3
Lines centered by a typesetting program don't always look centered. In the upper sample, the quotation marks and ellipse in the second line make that end of the line graphically weak, and the line seems off-center to the left. In the lower sample, the line has been nudged to the right by adding an en space before *Dr.*, and the line looks correctly centered.

Optical Alignment in Display Type

As point size increases, the graphic qualities of individual letters become more assertive. As a result, text that looks well aligned in text sizes looks out of whack at display sizes.

In flush-left display type, the starting points of lines should be adjusted to take this into account. In very large sizes (60-point and up) the side-bearings of the letters create noticeable indents on the left-hand margin. In such cases, display type may have to extend outside the left-hand margin to have it appear flush-left.

With sans serif display types, letters with square shapes on their left-hand sides (such as F, r, h) should set flush against the left-hand margin. But letters with round (O, c, s) or angled shapes (A, Y, x) should be allowed to extend slightly beyond the margin to make them appear flush left. The same is true with drop caps, in which letters with nonsquare left-side shapes may have to extend beyond the margin to appear correctly aligned. Obliqued sans serif faces should all be treated like angled characters to achieve proper optical alignment.

In flush-left serifed display type, the left-side serifs of most letters should be allowed to extend slightly beyond the left hand margin. Otherwise, the rules for alignment are same as with sans serif faces.

Optical Vertical Centering Between Rules

Text that's mechanically centered vertically between rules—which is common in table or chart headings—rarely looks correct. If the rules and the type sandwiched between them are all on the same leading, the type will look too high (see Figure 2.4). In all-caps text, this effect is even more exaggerated.

In all-caps text, though, the problem is easier to fix. You simply measure the total white space above and below the text and divide it evenly between top and bottom. As seen in Figure 2.4, this results in the type sitting on a leading almost exactly twice that of the lower rule, with the sum of the two leading amounts being the distance between the baselines of the two rules.

In upper-and-lowercase copy, the text needs to be nudged about

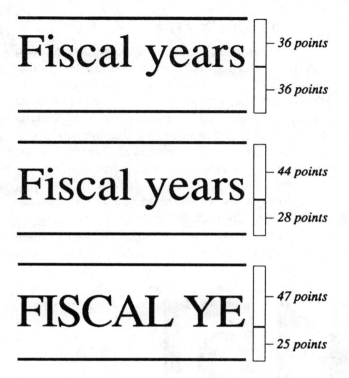

Figure 2.4
Type has to be centered visually when set between rules. When the rules and the type are set on the same leading, as in the top sample, the type appears too high. Because caps-and-lowercase text is more bottom-heavy than all-caps text, it needs to be set slightly higher when placed between rules, as seen in the bottom two samples.

10 percent higher than it would in all-caps copy to appear centered.

Because centering is an optical, not a mathematical, proposition, these relationships may vary slightly from case to case. Text set in all initial caps (up style) will tend to look higher than normal caps-and-lowercase (down-style text).

Character Alignment in Display Type

Some characters that look fine at text sizes may look misaligned in display sizes. Parentheses and brackets, for instance, are designed to encompass the entire body of the type, from ascender line to descender line. This makes them look too low when set with text that has no descenders, such as all-caps text and numerals. This is particularly obvious in display type, especially when setting telephone numbers. To correct this problem, you may elect to center parentheses and brackets on cap height when using them in display sizes, as shown in Figure 2.5.

The same applies to hyphens, which are designed to center on x-height, because they're usually used in lower-case text. Hyphens appear too low when set in all-cap text. You may prefer to raise them up to center on cap-height.

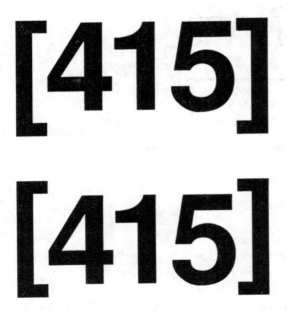

Figure 2.5
When parentheses and brackets are used in display sizes, they seem misaligned in numeric or all-caps copy, as seen in the upper sample. Below, the brackets have been raised to center on cap height for a more natural, balanced look.

Specifying Type

The person setting type needs to be given all the typographic specifications, and these should be communicated in a clear and consistent style. The most important of these are:

Typeface
Point size
Leading
Measure
Margin treatment (justified or ragged)
Indention
Tracking of large display type

Typeface

The name of the desired typeface is best spelled out, and not abbreviated. Use the complete name of the typeface, as not all typeface names are trademarked, and versions of some classic faces with the same basic name are distributed by various type foundries. Simply specifying Bodoni, for example, could lead to confusion among Linotype Bodoni, Monotype Bodoni, Bitstream Bodoni, Casady & Greene Bodoni, and Kingsley/ATF Bodoni, among others.

Because desktop fonts can be customized by their owners (through the addition of custom kerning pairs, for instance) even two Bodoni fonts from the same manufacturer may not be identical. If you are working on a document formatted by someone else, make sure that you have fonts identical to those used by the originator. If the fonts used in the two versions of the document are not identical, line endings may vary, altering the layout of the document. (See Kerning in Chapter 1 for more on controlling letter spacing.)

Always specify the typeface's weight and style, such as Times Roman Bold or Helvetica Light Condensed Italic. A type sample book will contain the full names of a manufacturer's typefaces.

In familiar situations, where abbreviation is not apt to cause confusion, some short forms of type face names are often used:

Hel Bold Ital (or even HBI)	*means*	Helvetica Bold Italic
Century SB	*means*	Century Schoolbook
Goudy OS	*means*	Goudy Old Style

Point Size and Leading

Point size refers to the height of the typeset letters, and leading refers to the amount of space between successive lines of type, as measured from baseline to baseline.

When specifying type, point size and leading are almost always expressed together, and the two values are typically written separated by a slash:

| 10/10 | *means* | 10-point type on 10-point leading |
| 12/14 | *means* | 12-point type on 14-point leading |

When point size and leading are equal, the setting is referred to as *solid.* This refers to handset type, when no additional lead was added between rows of letters, so the point size of the type was also the distance between lines of type.

| 12' solid | *means* | 12-point type on 12-point leading |

Measure and Margin Treatment

These two specifications are also typically stated together. The *measure*, or line length, is specified in picas and points. The margins of a column of type can be set *ragged* (where not all lines completely fill the measure) or *justified* (where all lines fill the measure completely). For more on margin treatments, see Margin Styles in this chapter.

To be clear, it's always best to state explicitly how both margins should be treated. Use the terms *justified, flush-left/ragged-right, flush-right/ragged-left*, and *centered.* For brevity, the word *rag* is often used in place of *ragged* in these descriptions, hence *flush-left/rag-right*, and so forth.

The following abbreviations are commonly used when writing instructions for how margins should be specified:

FL *or* RR *or* FL/RR	*means*	flush-left/ragged-right
FR *or* RL *or* FR/RL	*means*	flush-right/ragged-left
J *or* FL/FR	*means*	justified
C	*means*	centered

A common shorthand method for writing descriptions of margins and measures is to use brackets and squiggly lines to indicate flush and ragged margins respectively, with the measure placed between the two symbols. For instance,

[24.6⟩	*means*	flush-left, ragged-right, over a 24½ pica measure
⟩24.6]	*means*	flush-right, ragged-left, over a 24½ pica measure
[24.6]	*means*	justified over a 24½ pica measure
]24.6[	*means*	centered over a 24½ pica measure

Another shorthand method uses the initials of the margin treatment and a multiplication sign to indicate the line length:

| 10/12 Bembo RR × 16 | *means* | 10-point Bembo on 12-point leading set ragged-right over a 16-pica measure |

Indention

The most commonly overlooked typographic specification is the depth of the paragraph indent. This can be specified in points, picas and points, or in ems and ens. The depth of a paragraph indent should be proportional to the type size and measure being used. A very shallow paragraph indent on a wide line of type does not provide the necessary degree of graphic punctuation. Too deep an indent can cause a page of type to look fractured. One-em, two-em, and three-em paragraph indents in narrow, medium, and wide measures respectively are common norms. (See Indention Style in this chapter for details.)

The depths of hanging indents and right and left indents should also be specified clearly and consistently. To avoid having to mark every indent in a manuscript, specify the size of the first example to occur and add the word *typical* or *global* to indicate that all succeeding occurrences of a similar indent should be treated the same way.

Display Type Spacing

Large display type is typically letterspaced more tightly than text type. The spacing between the individual letters in large type should be reduced because the eye perceives large type to be more loosely set than small type, even though it's set with the same spacing specifications of smaller point sizes. (For more on tracking, letterspacing, and kerning, see Chapter 1.) Without specifying numeric values for the spacing of display type, the tightness of display type is usually described in one of three ways (shown in Figure 2.6):

Normal

Spacing

Tight but not touching

Spacing

Tight

Spacing

Figure 2.6
Of the three standard degrees of character spacing in display type, the "normal" setting is the most common. Even this setting, though, is substantially tighter than that of type set at text sizes.

The "tight-but-not-touching" setting is often used in magazine and display type. But the "tight" setting is rarely seen outside of advertising type.

Normal—This is tighter than the set of the text type it accompanies, but this setting provides the same optical sense of spacing as that found in the smaller type.

Tight but not touching—This is a common setting used in advertising, where tight letterspacing in display type is widely accepted. It's also commonly used in magazine display type and logos. Despite its name, in type specified this way there may be occasional contact between adjoining characters.

Tight—This is very tightly set type. Ligatures (the touching or overlapping of adjoining letters) may occur frequently as letters are spaced as tightly but as evenly as possible. This style is most popular in advertising type but is inappropriate for most newspapers, books, magazines, and manuscripts.

Typeface Choice

Of the tens of thousands of typefaces available today, over 90 percent of texts are set in fewer than two dozen typefaces. By and large, these are variations on a few classic typefaces that have been in use since the Renaissance.

Typefaces are divided into two main categories, according to whether or not the letters have *serifs,* small counterstrokes that appear at the ends of the main strokes of a letter. Serifs make typefaces more legible, so almost all faces used for text, such as Times Roman, have serifs. *Sans serif* faces (from the French, *without serifs*) are more commonly used in applications other than running text.

Times Roman (serif)
Helvetica (sans serif)

Typefaces can be catalogued in a number of ways, but the most practical way is by their use.

Text faces are designed specifically for long passages of text, such as in books, magazines, and reports. They are almost exclusively serifed faces whose designs are not very assertive. A good text face is legible and attractive but does not draw attention to itself on the page.

Display faces are designed for use in large sizes, such as headlines and titles. They are also often used in text sizes for short passages, such as captions or bylines. Sans serif faces are commonly used as display faces, as are bold and extra bold versions of text faces. Display faces may have a more flamboyant design than text faces, and they tend to be used for emphasis rather than readability.

Decorative faces have a limited range of expression. They typically evoke historical eras or create arresting visual effects that are appropriate only on certain occasions. Their designs may be gimmicky, with letters constructed from paper clips, neon tubes, tree branches, or ribbons.

Typeface names can be confusing. Many of the classic names cannot be copyrighted, so there are many variations of such faces as Garamond and Baskerville that have similar or identical names. The following short list represents some of the most popular and commonly used text faces using the names by which they are best known.

Baskerville
Bembo
Janson
Times Roman
Century Old Style
ITC Caslon
ITC Garamond
ITC Galliard
Plantin

Type faces are organized into families, typically combining roman and italic versions in a variety of weights. The weight of a typeface is a measure of the thickness of the strokes used to build the letters. Within a given family, for example Galliard, the face that simply bears the name of the family is generally the weight intended for use in text. Occasionally, the text version of a face is labelled as book weight, as in ITC Garamond Book. Avoid using any weights but these for text because lighter or heavier weights are not as readable.

A large family of type may contain the following weights, listed here in ascending order:

Thin
Light

Regular (or Book)
Medium
Demibold
Bold
Heavy
Extra Bold
Black
Extra Black

As a rule, only regular, book, and medium make good text faces. The bolder members of a typeface family are useful for display type, captions, and call-outs (attention-getting devices), where the text is short and its graphical role is emphasized.

Large typeface families may have members whose characters have been designed to be narrower than normal. These faces are called *condensed* or *compressed*. These are not the same faces you get if you use your computer to compress a regular-width face. In true condensed type, the proportions of the characters have been reworked to be most legible in their reduced widths. When possible, use a true condensed face, rather than condensing it yourself electronically.

Similarly, some faces also have *expanded* versions, which, like their condensed relatives, have been designed specifically for legibility at their new widths. Avoid using condensed or expanded faces for long passages of text. Reserve them for display roles, captions, call-outs, and so on.

The Page Grid

The *grid* of a page is the underlying structure that defines where text and graphic elements on the page align. The grid, as created by a graphic designer, assures design consistency from page to page and makes page assembly easier by specifying standard points at which repeating page elements should be positioned. Documents whose pages are printed on both sides have distinct left- and right-hand page grids, which typically mirror each other.

The page grid is divided vertically into columns. These may or may not correspond to the number of text columns on your the page. The simple grid illustrated in Figure 2.7 shows how a 6-column grid can be used to lay out 2- or 3-column pages. The more columns a grid contains, the more flexible and versatile (and potentially confusing) it becomes.

In addition to defining the positions of text columns and the *gutters* of white space between them, the columns of a grid also provide horizontal alignment and positioning guides for illustrations, display type, and other page elements.

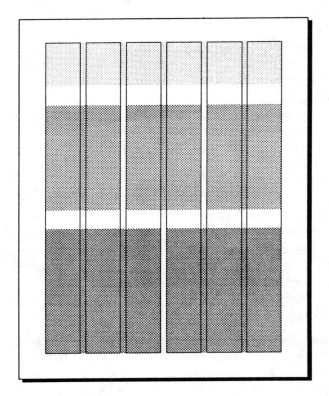

Figure 2.7
This simple six-column grid is quite versatile. As shown here, it can be used for one-, two- or three-column pages. It can also be used for asymmetrical pages, in which the main text is 4-columns wide, and marginal copy such as captions and notes can be set two columns wide.

Crossing the columns at right angles are horizontal *grid lines* that serve as vertical alignment guides. These may be *hang lines* (top-alignment points from which graphic elements such as photographs hang like laundry) or baselines (upon which text or graphics sit). The entire printed area of a page is often crossed with grid lines whose spacing corresponds to the leading used in the main text. In this case, the top margin of the page (grid line 0) would act as a hang line, from which, for example, a heavy rule may descend to form the page's top border. From there to the bottom of the page, vertical positions can be specified by a grid-line number.

Simple page grids may need very few horizontal grid lines. Vertical positions that should be specified include the following:

Top and bottom margins
Positions of running heads and feet
Top display-type baseline
Top text baseline for opening pages (those with display type)
Top text baseline for following pages

Special Characters

Type fonts offer a wide range of characters not available on a traditional keyboard, and typesetting has its own rules for how even the familiar old typewriter characters are used.

Spacing of Symbols and Pi Characters

Symbols *Followed* by a Space:

@
©
® (when used at full size)
• (and all symbols used to highlight listed items)
§
¶

Symbols *Preceded* and *Followed* by Spaces:

&
+, −, =, ×, ÷, ≈, ≠, <, >, ≤, ≥ (when used in formulas)

Symbols *Not Followed* by a Space:

#

$

±

+ (when used to indicate an increase, such as +40%, or a positive value, such as +40° Fahrenheit.

− (minus, when used in the same sense as as + above)

Symbols *Not Preceded* by a Space:

%, ‰

* (asterisk)

¢

×(when used to indicate powers of magnitude, as in a 3× increase or a 40× power telescope)

° (degree symbol)

® (when used as a superior after text)

TM

′ ″(primes)

Symbols Set *Closed-Up*, Without Spaces Before or After:

- (hyphen, except in cases such as *first- and second-class tickets*)

– (en dash)

— (em dash)

Hyphens and Dashes

Hyphens and en dashes are connecting forms of punctuation. Em dashes are used to separate parts of a text.

Use hyphens to connect compound words and to divide words at the end of typeset lines.

Do not use a hyphen as a minus sign; it's too short. (See Mathematical Symbols, below.)

Use en dashes to indicate ranges of numbers:

1945–52
pages 67–99

Don't break lines after en dashes used in this way.

Use en dashes in compound hyphenated words. When a word contains two hard hyphens, the second should be replaced with an en dash:

a run-in–style index

Em dashes indicate a break in the thought or structure of a sentence. Em dashes may be used—in a manner similar to parentheses—to set off a phrase or comment that appears midsentence.

An em dash is an acceptable breaking point for a line of type. An em dash that appears at the end of a line should not be followed by a hyphen.

Parentheses, Brackets, and Braces

Parentheses are used to set off explanatory, digressive, or emphatic comments from the main text. Text surrounded by parentheses is not separated from them by word spaces.

When the last word inside roman parentheses is set in italic, make sure that the last letter doesn't touch the closing parenthesis. Kern this character combination manually, if necessary, to avoid the contact.

Brackets ([ ]) are used to enclose parenthetical matter in text inside parentheses:

(Sources confirmed that Dottie [Mrs. Eugene] Brown was in attendance.)

Brackets are used to enclose editorial comments and amendments to text:

The senator said, "If Ben [Smythe] wants it, he can have it!"

Brackets are used to enclose the word *sic* (thus) to indicate that an apparent error is a correct representation of the text as originally written or spoken:

"*As Macbeth [sic] said, 'Something's rotten in Denmark.'*"

Braces ({ }) are mainly used for setting mathematical formulas. They may also be used in lists and tables to indicate that a number of entries share a common heading, price, etc.

Ligatures

Ligatures are pairs of letters fused into one character. Sometimes ligatures are formed to accommodate the shapes of letters. The *f/i* (fi) and *f/l* (fl) ligatures have been created because the hook of the *f* tends to collide with tall letters that follow it. Likewise, *f/f/l* (ffl) and *f/f/i* (ffi) ligatures exist in some fonts.

Other ligatures—notably *o/e* (œ, Œ) and *a/e* (æ, Æ) represent diphthongs, distinct vowel sounds. These diphthong ligatures that appear in some historic contexts are archaic usages that sometimes still appear in words such as encylopædia. They are also commonly used in Scandinavian languages.

Except in very loosely set matter, where the letter *f* doesn't touch adjoining letters, use ligatures as a matter of course in running text. Do not use ligatures in display type, except for diphthong ligatures, which may be necessary for editorial or grammatical reasons.

If your composition program automatically inserts ligatures, it should be able to substitute the spelled out forms when spacing specifications call for a word like raffle to be hyphenated. If you have to add ligatures manually (through a search-and-replace procedure, for example) the rare occasion may arise that a ligature will prevent desired hyphenation.

Points of Ellipsis

Points of ellipsis indicate the omission of text. When the omission occurs midsentence, the ellipsis consists of three consecutive periods (. . .) with a full space between the periods and between the periods and the text.

When it occurs at the end of a sentence, a fourth, sentence-ending period is added. If the sentence in question is complete, this fourth period is set closed-up against the final character like a normal period:

> *The Declaration of Independence states we are "... dedicated to the proposition that all men are created equal...."*

If the sentence is not complete, the four periods of the ellipse are separated from the text by a word space:

> *"... endowed by their Creator with certain unalienable rights...."*

Many fonts contain an ellipsis character (...), but because its periods are very tightly spaced, this should be reserved for use in display type only, where tighter spacing is the rule. In text, this narrow ellipsis is not emphatic enough. In addition, this character cannot be converted into a four-period ellipse.

You can make a better ellipse manually, using periods and nonbreaking spaces. A *nonbreaking space* (offered by most text processing and composition programs) is the same width as a word space, but it is not a legal line-breaking point. An ellipse in which the periods are linked with nonbreaking spaces will move as a unit during composition and not be divided at a line break.

An ellipse may appear at the beginning of a line or at the end of a line of type, but it should not be allowed to appear by itself as a widow. To prevent this, an ellipse at the end of a paragraph should be joined to the word it follows by a nonbreaking space.

Superscripts and Subscripts

Superscripts and subscripts (also called *superiors* and *inferiors*) are most commonly used for footnotes, fractions, chemical formulas, and mathematical equations. Most composition programs enable you to define the size of these characters, with the standard size ranging from 60 percent to 70 percent of the normal text.

Superscripts should top-align with the ascenders of the text with which they're used. Subscripts should center on the baseline—that is, the baseline should pass midway through inferior characters.

Superscripts for footnotes should be set outside of the punctuation in a sentence:

Martin Luther married late in life.[1]

Mathematical superscripts should be set inside the punctuation:

His formula states, $a^2 = b^2 + c^2$.

Mathematical Symbols

The use of mathematical symbols is complicated by the fact that, as of this writing, most desktop publishing programs do not provide easy access to minus (–) and multiplication (x) signs. This is because these characters are missing from the standard Apple character set. These symbols exist in most common pi fonts, though, including the PostScript Symbol font.

When used in formulas or mathematical statements, common math symbols should be flanked by word spaces:

2 + 2 = 4

When a math symbol is used as a prefix or suffix for a numeral, it should not be set with any intervening word space:

+20%
a 2x increase

A minus sign is a distinct typographical symbol. It is longer than a hyphen and shorter than an en dash, and neither of these symbols should be substituted for it:

-20° C. (with a hyphen)
–20° C. (with a minus sign)
—20° C. (with an en dash)

A multiplication sign is also a distinct typographical symbol. Don't use an *x* in place of a multiplication sign. If you don't want to use the multiplication sign in expressions of measurement, spell out the phrase:

8½ × 11" paper

or:

8¹/₂-by-11-inch paper

not:

8¹/₂ x 11" paper

Except in tables and scientific matter, spell out *times* rather than using ×:

profits increased by five times over last year

or:

a five-fold increase in profits over last year

not:

a 5× increase in profits over last year

Primes

Primes are used to indicate inches and feet and minutes and seconds. A single prime is also used to express typographical points. Primes, like the minus sign, are not included in many fonts, but italicized typewriter-style quotation marks make excellent substitutes:

Height: 5'4" (set with primes)
Height: 5' 4" (set with italicized typewriter-style quotations marks)

Dotless i

The dotless i (ı) is used to create accented characters such as î and ï. Because these characters are now included in most fonts or can be built automatically by composition programs, the dotless i is now most commonly used in tightly spaced display type.

Ligatures are not used in display type, so the dotless i may be used in situations where the dot would otherwise collide with part of an adjoining letter, most commonly the *f*. It may also be used when an *i* appears next to other overhanging letters, such as *T*, *P*, and *F*.

Names and Uses of International Characters

The following punctuation marks and symbols are used for international typesetting work and are found in most electronic fonts:

Guillemets (« » ‹ ›)

Guillemets are used as quotation marks in some European languages. Unlike quotation marks, they are separated slightly from the text they enclose.

Spanish Question Mark, Exclamation Point (¿ ¡)

The Spanish language uses inverted question marks and exclamation points as the first characters in interrogatory and exclamatory sentences respectively. They are set without a word space following them.

Feminine and Masculine Ordinal Superiors (ª º)

Used in Romance languages such as Spanish and Italian, these characters are set after a numeral to make it an ordinal number. The word *primero* (*first*), for example, may be abbreviated 1º, and *seconda* may be abbreviated 2ª. French ordinals (such as 1ere and 2eme) are not included in standard font character sets.

Accents and Accented Characters

Most current computer type fonts contain a full set of accented characters for setting most European languages. (In older composition systems accented characters were created manually by superimposing an accent character over a letter.) The accents available in these fonts for both lowercase and capital letters are:

â	circumflex
ö	diaeresis, or umlaut
ñ	tilde
è	grave accent
é	acute accent

ç   cedilla
ø   Scandinavian accented *o*
å   ring accent

Avoid solid leading in material with accented capitals. Add extra lead to prevent these accents from colliding with descenders in the lines above them.

Common Pi Characters

The most common use for pi characters is to highlight listed items. Characters used this way are generically called bullets. (Lists highlighted this way are called bulleted lists). True bullets, though, are round (see below). When used as bullets, pi characters or *dingbats* (typographical ornaments, such as flowers, snowflakes, and leaves) should be separated by a word space from the text they highlight. Bulleted lists are most effective when the bullets are separated from the text by using a hanging indent (see Indention Style in Chapter 2).

Most pi characters come in solid (filled-in) and open (hollow, or outline) styles. Avoid decorative dingbats such as indexes (☞), stars (★), and checks (✔), unless you want to draw attention to the symbols themselves. If you want to draw attention to a passage of text, use one of the simple geometric shapes below.

Bullets (•)

Bullets come in several sizes, typically half-x-height, x-height, and cap-height. For use in highlighting listed items, use x-height bullets, which are suitably sized for this role. Half-x-height bullets are not emphatic enough, and cap-height bullets are too large and distracting. Cap-height and x-height bullets should center on cap height. When used with lowercase text, half-x-height bullets should be centered on x-height.

Ballot Box (□)

As its name implies, the ballot box in its open form is used in check-off forms, such as coupons and ballots. A solid ballot box is sometimes called a square bullet and is used in the same ways as a round, solid bullet. Ballot boxes come in the same sizes as bullets and align like bullets. When a ballot box is used for check-off purposes, it should be set cap-height or slightly larger and sit on the baseline. A larger, full-body-size ballot box is also often used for this purpose.

Triangles (▲)

Solid triangles are useful alternatives to round and square bullets in highlighting list entries. When used in this capacity, they should be rotated to point toward the copy. Triangles used in this role are most effective when set cap-height and centered on cap height.

Character Style

This chapter looks at the style of individual type characters—how individual letters should be set and formatted. This combines elements of copyediting style and standard typographic practice. When setting type or composing pages, you may be working with manuscripts prepared by a number of authors and editors, not all of whom agree on basic copyediting conventions. And most won't know many of the rules of typography. As the person composing the type, then, you'll often become the arbiter of style.

Numerals, Numbers, Dates, and Fractions

General Rules

Don't start a sentence with a numeral or a date. Rewrite sentences to avoid this whenever possible.

Don't use old-style numbers in tables and financial reports.

1234567890

Old-style figures aren't all the same height and don't all align on the baseline, so they can disrupt clean alignment in tabular matter.

When to Spell Out Numbers

In general, spell out numbers from 0 to 100:

All forty-five delegates from Georgia stormed out.
Will Puerto Rico become the fifty-first state?

In general, set numbers of 100 or more as numerals.

Ordinals follow the same rule:

Fifth Avenue, not 5th Avenue
First base, not 1st base

When a series of numbers would become too long and confusing to spell out, use numerals:

His brothers are aged 45, 47, 52, 55, and 61.

Spell out numbers in situations such as:

I've told him a hundred times.

not:

I've told him 100 times.

Spell out large, round numbers:

The crowd numbered ten thousand.

Use numbers consistently within a passage; specific numbers determine the style of other numbers *used in the same sense* in the same sentence:

Ajax Corp. grew from 140 employees to over 1,000 in eight months.

not:

Ajax Corp. grew from 140 employees to over a thousand in eight months.

and:

Ajax Corp. grew from about 20 employees to 150 in eight months.

not:

Ajax Corp. grew from about twenty employees to 150 in eight months.

For spelling purposes, numeric expressions are divided into scientific (including statistical) and nonscientific applications. In general, numerals are used in scientific texts where they would otherwise be spelled out in nonscientific texts:

The samples were 45 microns apart.
Grandmother lives forty-five miles away.
The samples were preserved at a temperature of 20°.
The high temperature today was only twenty degrees.

But even in nonscientific texts, when numbers are used for statistical purposes, such as specifying quantities or measurements, numerals should be used:

The poll indicated that 23 percent of the voters approved.

Use the percentage sign only in tables and scientific copy:

Adding a 55% solution corrected the acid balance.

In nonscientific, nonstatistical text, spell out *percent,* but not the number:

The mortgage interest rate is 12 percent.

Spell out isolated money references: *fifty dollars, ten cents.* In general, don't use the cents (¢) sign, and don't use figures such as $.50, except in tables.

Ranges of Numbers

Use en dashes to indicate ranges of numbers:

pages 44–56
the years 1865–1902

When expressing ranges in this way, some numerals may be omitted in the second number.

From 1–99, both numbers set completely:

22–27

From 100–109 (or any such three-digit number), the first two numerals may be dropped in the second number:

101–8

In other three-digit numbers, only the repeating first numeral should be omitted:

561–69

Likewise,

1940–45

In ranges of four digit numbers, such as dates, where only the first numeral is common to both numbers, all numerals in the second number should be set:

1885–1922

When expressing ranges in text, using an en dash preempts the use of the words *from* and *to:*

He worked during the years 1922–36.

or:

He worked during the years from 1922 to 1936.

not:

He worked during the years from 1922–36.

Dates

When dates are written in the month/day/year format, the year is preceded and followed by commas:

June 4, 1951, is a historic day.

not:

June 4, 1951 is a historic day.

To eliminate the commas, the day/month/year format is sometimes used, but it tends to look odd to American readers:

The date 4 June 1951 is historic.

When the day is eliminated, so is the need for the comma:

He was born in June 1951.

Days of the months should be written as cardinals, not ordinals:

June 4 is an important day.

not:

June 4th is an important day.

However, after a specific date has been cited as a cardinal, a following related date may be spelled out as an ordinal number:

He was born on June 4, but he wasn't named until the seventh.

Avoid using slashes or hyphens to abbreviate dates (*6/4/51 or 6-4-51*), because their meanings are ambiguous. In the U.S., such an expression reflects a month/day/year format, but outside the U.S., it more often translates as day/month/year.

When setting years using numerals, use an apostrophe only to indicate that numerals have been omitted:

He grew up during the '60s.
The migrations occurred in the 1880s.

References to centuries should be spelled out and not capitalized:

The country grew rapidly in the nineteenth century.

When years are specified as A.D., this label precedes the date:

The battle was in A.D. 1066.

When years are specified as B.C., B.C.E., or A.C.E., this label follows the date:

Julius Caesar died in 44 B.C.

Fraction Style

The typographic style of fractions should be consistent throughout a document. Some fonts include preconfigured, or prebuilt, fractions in their character sets. But if you use these, make sure that you use them for all the fractions in your document. It's almost impossible to build a fraction, or have your program build it for you, that will look exactly like the prebuilt fractions. If you have to build one fraction, for the sake of consistency you should build them all,

A properly built fraction should use numerators and denominators that are between 60 and 70 percent of the size of the surrounding text. The numerator should top-align with the text—that is, the top of the numerator should be at the same height as the tops of the capitals or ascending letters of the surrounding text. The denominator should sit on the baseline.

Use the *fraction bar* character for building fractions, not the *slash* (also called a *virgule* or *solidus*) character found on your keyboard. The fraction bar is designed to provide better spacing between itself and the numerator and denominator. However, you may have to adjust the spacing of the numerator and denominator relative to the fraction bar to get a balanced-looking fraction (see the section, Kerning in Chapter 1).

In text that is nonscientific, and where fractions are casually used, spell out common fractions:

Two-thirds of the class voted against the rule.
He did the job in half the time.

Quantities that use a combination of integers and fractions should be set in numerals and built fractions:

8$\frac{1}{2}$-by-11-inch paper

Don't use "th" after fractions:

$\frac{1}{6}$ inch

not:

$\frac{1}{6}$th inch

Don't use *of* after measurement expressed in fractions:

$\frac{1}{6}$ inch

not:

$\frac{1}{6}$ of an inch

Write percents with decimals, not fractions:

25.5 percent

not:

25½ percent

Punctuation

This section deals almost exclusively with the typographic aspects of punctuation. For more information on correct use of punctuation, consult an editorial style guide, such as *The Chicago Manual of Style* (The University of Chicago Press) or *Words Into Type* (Prentice Hall). For a briefer overview, consult *The Elements of Style* (Macmillan).

Punctuation marks, including periods, commas, colons, and semicolons, should be followed by only one word space.

Hyphens and dashes should abut letters directly, without any intervening word spaces, except in split compound hyphenates, such as the following:

Only second- or third-rate works were selected.

Don't use the typewriter-style (neutral) quotation marks (' ") printed on your keyboard. Use their typographical equivalents, true opening (' ") and closing (' ") quotation marks. The single closing quote is the same as an apostrophe. Only use neutral quotes in creating ASCII manuscripts and when italicized quotes are substituted for primes (see Primes in Chapter 3).

Set periods and commas inside closing quotation marks:

"The problem," Marley said, "is Ebenezer's, not mine."

Use single quotation marks to enclose quotes within quotes:

She cried, "Why can't you say 'I love you'?"

Single quotation marks can also be used in place of italics to highlight special terms:

The term 'kerning' dates back hundreds of years.

Punctuation gets its typographic identity—italic or roman or bold— from the word or character it follows:

The word inflammable, *though correct, is too seldom used.*

Use apostrophes to form the plurals of abbreviations and single letters:

Mind your p's *and* q's.
M.D.'s and R.N.'s

Use quotation marks to enclose the titles of book chapters and articles in magazines and periodicals.

Abbreviations and Acronyms

Avoid abbreviations—spell out words if space permits. One common exception is *Inc.*, short for *Incorporated.* Common business abbreviations such as *1st Q '93* should be spelled out:

By the first quarter of 1993 we expect improvements.

Don't use word spaces in an abbreviation with internal periods:

Q. Jackson Lawrence, Ph.D.

Use spaces after the periods when a person's initials are used:

E. M. Forster

The Latin abbreviations *e.g.* (*exempli gratia*, for example) and *i.e.* (*id est*, that is) are always followed by a comma:

Small mammals (e.g., mice) are commonly preyed upon.

Set acronyms without periods:

NAACP
AFL-CIO
NORAD

The following commonly accepted abbreviations for time are set with periods and in small caps (although A.M. and P.M. are often set in lowercase):

9:45 A.M.
1:00 P.M.
A.D. 1864
504 B.C.

Although midnight (*12:00 P.M.*) and noon (*12:00 M.*) have proper abbreviations, it's clearer to use the spelled-out forms.

The abbreviation *etc.* (*et cetera,* and so forth) must be followed by a comma if it appears midsentence. It should never be preceded by *and,* which is redundant. This abbreviation should appear at the end of no less than two things:

> *The shop sold hats, coats, etc.*

not:

> *The shop sold clothes, etc.*

Capitals and Small Caps

Capitals in Display Type

Headlines and titles are typically set in one of three ways:

> *Up style,* which uses initials capitals
> *Down style,* which capitalizes only the first word and proper nouns
> *Caps and small caps,* which uses small caps in place of lower-case letters

In up style titles, all words are capitalized except articles and prepositions:

> *The Effect of Gamma Rays on Man-in-the-Moon Marigolds*

Exceptions are where an article or preposition plays an important part in the text, where it is used as a proper modifier, or where a preposition is used as part of a verb:

> *Up the Down Staircase*
> *Suspect Arrested in The Bronx*
> *Court Knocks Down Poll Tax*

In up style text, longer prepositions (through, before, etc.) are often capitalized. If you choose to do this, do it consistently throughout the work.

In titles, both words in compound and hyphenated phrases should be capitalized:

Hot-Shot Lawyers Change Small-Town Zoning Laws

Small Capitals

The size of small capitals varies from typeface to typeface. Generally, small caps are about 70 percent of the height of the full-size capitals. The visual mass of text set in small caps must be in balance with the surrounding type. If the small caps are too small (e.g., x-height) they look out of balance. If they are too large (too close to the size of full-size capitals) they appear too massive and disrupt the color of the type, which defeats the purpose of using them in the first place.

There are a few instances where the use of small caps is standard. The most common of these are in abbreviations concerning time and historical reference points:

6:00 A.M.
5:30 P.M.
1,000,000 B.C.
A.D. 1066

It is becoming more common, though, to see *a.m.* and *p.m.* set in lowercase type.

Small capitals in display type may be set larger or smaller than small capitals in text, because legibility and type color are less crucial in headlines and titles.

When using small capitals together with full-size caps, pay close attention to letter spacing between full-size and small caps, where spacing tends to become too loose. To make sure that word spaces are of consistent size in such text, format all word spaces along with either the large or small caps. This assures that all the spaces between large and small caps will be of consistent size.

Small caps are often used following a drop cap that opens a paragraph (see Drop Caps and Standing Caps in Chapter 2). A phrase or full line in small caps helps to integrate the drop cap and the paragraph text.

Small caps are useful in setting headings for tables. They are more forceful than upper and lowercase text but don't take up as much space as full-size capitals.

When to Use Italics

Almost all text (like the text you're reading now) is set in regular-weight roman typefaces. There are a number of uses for italic type in roman text, some of which are mandated. But there are no standard uses for bold and bold italic type.

In general, keep the use of italic type to a minimum, because it's a bit more difficult to read than roman type. In addition, numerous changes of typeface are distracting to the reader.

Italics should be used for:

- Book titles
- Names of works of art, including musical compositions
- Names of films, plays, and television shows
- Titles of periodicals
- Newly introduced terms or technical terms ("This process is called *kerning.*")
- Definitions within a sentence ("His name in Hebrew means *peace.*")
- Names of ships and aircraft (H.M.S. *Beagle,* space shuttle *Challenger*)
- Single letters referred to as letters ("The letter *T* always needs kerning.")
- Genus and species ("It's the earliest example of *Homo sapiens.*")
- Foreign words and phrases that haven't been adopted into common usage. If in doubt, consult a dictionary, which will list many familiar foreign phrases and whether these should be set in roman or italic type. Generally, if it's not in the dictionary, set it in italics.

Most Latin words, phrases, and abbreviations are now commonly set in roman type, including circa (and its abbreviations c. and ca.), ante, post, ibid., et al., etc., and op. cit.

Possessive endings of words in italic should be set in roman ("They talked about the *New York Post*'s bankruptcy.")

Tables

Tables are a challenge for editors, designers, and typographers alike. The main thing to remember is that a table is a convenience for the reader. They are an "at-a-glance" resource used to find information quickly and easily. Therefore, tables should be simple, clean, and typographically precise, because the layout of a table is a key to its readability.

Table Terminology

Tables are divided into vertical columns or *tab fields*, the left-most of which is called the *stub*. Between adjacent columns lie gutters that separate adjacent tab entries. The overall width of a table, then, is the total of the widths of the tab fields and the gutters that separate them. One complete set of tab entries—from left margin to right—is called a tab cycle.

The labels that sit above tabular columns are called *headings*. When a group of subheadings are gathered together under a one heading, that main heading is called a *straddle head*.

Editorial Concerns

The text in a table doesn't just carry information. It also defines the structure of the table itself. Table text, then, should be as brief as possible. A table with concise entries is easier to read, and keeping copy brief makes the size of the table more manageable.

A table should have a clear focus and purpose. It shouldn't be a dumping ground for data that's too hard to describe in words. Nor should it attempt to be encyclopedic. The title should be clear and concise so readers know immediately what they're looking at.

Tables should allow the reader to make comparisons easily. Tables with many footnotes frustrate this goal. A lot of footnotes in a table is often a symptom of poor organization—too many exceptions undermine the organizational scheme of the table.

Keep table entries brief. When entries fit on one line, a table is neat and easy to follow. The exception is in the stub tab, the left-most column in the table, which contains the description or name of the things being compared in the rest of the columns. Still, stub entries should be brief, with no more than two turnover lines, if possible, or the rest of the table will become too airy. Remember that the longest tab entry defines the spacing for all the others in that row or column.

When writing the text for a table, keep its eventual size in mind. Don't create tables that have to be shoehorned into the page. Whenever possible, create tables with the same visual orientation as the other pages in document—avoid making the reader turn the page sideways to read a table.

For information that can help you to organize your tables, see "Specifying Table Structures" below.

Styles of Table Entries

The most effective tables are completely self-explanatory, so avoid using symbols or colors when a simple text entry will suffice. Some symbols, though, are universally recognized and can be used without explanation. For example, if your table compares the features of two products, you can safely use a check mark (✓) in place of a "Yes" to indicate the presence of a particular feature. In such a table, an empty space is generally taken to mean "No" (the feature is missing), as shown in Figure 5.1.

If a complex table calls for symbols to replace written entries, the meaning of the symbols should be self-evident or easy to remember.

COMPARING ECONOMY TVS

Model and Size	Cable-Ready	VCR Jack	Remote Control	Contrast Control	Tint Control	Hue Control	Auto-Tuning
Master Color Mark IV 19-inch color	✓	✓		✓	✓	✓	
Global Vision 21 21-inch color	✓	✓	✓		✓		✓
Mega Color II 27-inch color	✓		✓	✓	✓	✓	
Acme All-Band 21-inch black-&-white		✓	✓		—	—	✓
EconoTube 19-inch black-&-white	✓	✓	✓	✓	—	—	✓

Figure 5.1
The meaning of symbols in a table should be obvious. Here, the check marks clearly mean "yes," the product has the feature indicated. The absence of an entry signals "no." Em dashes are a standard way to indicate that there's no information for a particular tab entry, or that the comparison being made in other columns doesn't apply.

Avoid using too many symbols or symbols that are so abstract that the reader has to refer constantly to a key or legend to figure out their meanings. This hampers the reader's ability to make comparisons between column entries.

Avoid mixing symbols and text entries in the same table. In a table like the product comparison mentioned above, if columns include text or numerical entries, the table will look better if you spell out "Yes" and "No."

An em dash is used to indicate that there is no data for that particular tab entry. Ellipses have also been used for this purpose, but this is out of style in contemporary design.

Use the abbreviation *n/a* or *N.A.* when data for a particular entry is not available. These abbreviations are also used to mean "not applicable," but to avoid any possible confusion, it's better to use an em dash for this purpose.

Kinds of Tab Programs

Tabs created in word processing programs (as well as many desktop publishing programs) are not the same as the tabs used in professional typesetting systems. Professional typographic tabs define columns with hard margins, just like those in multicolumn text pages. And as in a normal text column, when a line of text reaches the right-hand margin of a typographic tab column, it will break automatically and continue on the next line. As long as you continue typing, the text will continue to wrap, and the tab entry will become deeper and deeper.

Word-processor–style tabs, by contrast, merely indicate alignment points (called *tab stops*) on the page (see Figure 5.2). There are no hard margins in word processor–style tabs, so lines of text will not break until they hit the overall right-hand margin of the page, even if that means the type continues through other tab stops.

In word processor–style tabs, you hit the Tab key to advance the cursor from one tab stop to the next. This has the effect of pushing any text to the right of the cursor along with it. In typographic tabs, though, moving from tab to tab affects the cursor location only—the position of the text is not affected.

The power of typographic tabs is the control they give you over alignment of tab entries. For example, if you're typing a tab entry that's several lines deep, for example, advancing the cursor to the next tab field will automatically place the cursor on the same baseline as the first line of the tab entry you just completed. Likewise, at the end of a tab cycle, when you jump back to the stub column, the cursor will automatically move to a baseline below that of the deepest entry in the previous tab cycle. In addition, if later you need to change the widths of any or all of the tabs, the program will automatically adjust all the alignments to the new specifications. The hard-margined tab columns assure that when tab column widths change all tab entries will rerag within their proper columns and all alignments will be preserved.

If your program can't create these hard-margined tabs, there are two courses open to you. The first is to avoid creating tables with multiple-line tab entries, or at least keep them to a minimum. The second is to use a page composition program to create a multiple-column page, with each column serving as a column in your table. The advantage of doing this is that you have hard-margined columns and gutters like those in typographic tabs systems. With this strategy, you have to make all vertical alignments by hand, but editing text and

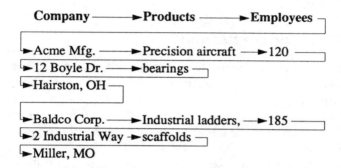

Tabbing sequence for word-processor tabs

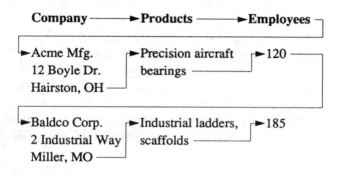

Figure 5.2

The upper diagram shows the complicated tabbing sequence required to align a simple table when using word-processor–style tabs. With such tabs, the only way to create multiple-line entries is to break them up over several lines. Editing a table like this is a headache because the lines of a multiple-line tab entry aren't contiguous—they're separated by other text and other Tab commands.

Below, you can see that in a typographic tab program, each tab entry is a complete unit. The text is typed in one piece within the tab column no matter how many lines deep it is. When one tab entry is finished, moving the cursor to the next tab brings it up to the same baseline as the one where the previous entry started. Likewise, at the end of a tab cycle, the cursor automatically drops down to a baseline below the deepest entry in the previous cycle.

tab widths is simplified because the text can rerag and at least remain in the appropriate "tab" column.

Specifying Table Structures

When a table sits above or below text on a one-column page, it is generally set to the same measure as the text. In multicolumn pages, you have the option of setting the table's measure at some multiple of the width of one column. Tables set within a column of text (that is, with text above and below the table) are typically indented slightly from both margins.

The widths of the entries in the stub tab define the amount of space left over for the other columns. As much as possible, use the widths of column entries to determine column widths, rather than allowing the widths of the column to be defined by their headings. Wide headings and narrow entries create a loose and airy table.

Some composition programs enable you to create *proportional tabs*. In these, you define the overall width of the table, the number of columns, the widths of the gutters, and the program then automatically divides the available space into columns of equal width. Similarly, some programs will create proportional tabs based on the width of the widest line of text in the stub tab. After figuring the width of the stub tab, the rest of the space is divided equally among the other columns.

Proportional tabs work best when the all the column entries are approximately the same width. When column entries vary too much in width, it's best to adjust the widths of the tab fields visually in order to balance the amount of white space that appears between columns.

In addition to tabs and gutter widths, you must also define how tab entries will align both horizontally (how the text is composed within the tab column) and vertically (how the vertical position of a tab entry relates to those on its left and right). Horizontal alignment choices include justified, ragged right, ragged left, centered, and decimal-aligned (for numerical entries, in which entries are aligned so that decimal points stack one over the other). Text set in tabs should almost always be set flush-left/rag-right. Numbers should be decimal-aligned. If there are no decimal points, you can simply set numbers flush right. When possible, avoid hyphenation in tab entries, even if tab-field measures are quite narrow.

Multiple-line tab entries must also align vertically. Typically, all entries within the same tab cycle start on the same baseline; that is, they *top-align*. A common exception is the text used for column headings, which is often set to bottom align, so that all entries in that cycle end on the same baseline. Advanced typesetting programs can also center-align tab entries, so that a four-line entry, for example, would start one line higher and finish one line deeper than a two-line entry in the tab field next to it, as seen in Figure 5.3. Center-aligned tabs are not very commonly used.

Product and Manufacturer	Rated Speed, in Pages per Minute	Time Between Repairs, in Months	Warrantee Coverage
SpotFlash 300 Lightning Printer Co.	8	10.25	Moving parts 90 days; electronics 1 yr.
QwikLaser 10 Qwik Corp.	10	16.0	All parts 6 mo.
LightWrite II LitePen Ltd.	14	8.1	All parts, 8 mo.

Figure 5.3
This simple table illustrates several things:
- Entries in the third column have been decimal aligned, so the decimal points stack vertically over each other no matter how many decimal places the numbers may extend to.
- The exterior rules of the table are heavier than the interior rule—a common configuration. In this case, the rule underneath the headings is a hairline.
- The heading in the stub column has been vertically centered relative to the other headings, which are all bottom-aligned.
- The heading in the fourth column has been indented to the left to visually center it over the flush-left column entries below it.

Spacing in Tables

Vertical Spacing

If you create tables in a word processor or page composition program that lacks hard-margined tabs (see Kinds of Tab Programs above), alignment will be easier if the leading is consistent throughout the table and all extra leading is added in full line spaces.

In a table with multiple-line tab entries, leading should be kept tight (solid or +1 point) for the sake of any runovers that appear. To keep horizontal rows distinct from each other in such a table, add a line space after each tab cycle.

In tables with single-line tab entries, the leading should be set wider. Make the leading 1½ to two times the point size of the type, with line spaces added between tab cycles, except between the column headings and the first tab cycle.

In very wide tables, an extra line space can be added when the entries in the stub tab make it logical to do so. If the stub tab contains subheadings, for instance, add a line space after the last of a series of subheadings and before the next main heading. The occasional extra line space will make the table easier to read across.

If your program handles tab alignment automatically, or if you don't mind a little extra work, the line spaces mentioned above can be converted into half-line spaces. A half-line space is enough to keep the tab cycles distinct from each other, and the tighter spacing creates a tighter-looking table and saves a little space on the page.

Indention

Most tab entries should be set flush left, without any indention. When entries in the stub tab are organized with subheadings and even sub-subheadings, these should be progressively indented, as in in standard outline style. Progressive en or em indents are typical.

Within tab entries, first-line indents are not used. Sometimes, though, they are set with hanging indents, with the first line set flush left within the tab, and successive lines indented by an en or em.

Optical Centering

Getting tabular entries to appear properly aligned can be difficult. Centered tab entries under flush-left headings tend to look off-center, as do decimal-aligned entries, especially when the length of the numbers varies greatly. Column headings under straddle heads also tend to appear off-center. Even flush-left tab entries can look unbalanced when they are much narrower or wider than the heading they sit under. In all these cases, even though the elements are correctly aligned mechanically, you should make individual adjustments to get them to look properly aligned.

Figure 5.4 shows some examples of how headings and columns may have to be indented or moved to create a balanced table. For more on this optical alignment, see Mechanical Alignment in Chapter 2.

Rules and Leaders in Tables

The rule on table rules is, the fewer, the better. Rely on the white space between columns and lines to guide the reader's eye around the table. However, a rule is commonly used to separate the headings from the column entries beneath them.

In very wide financial tables, rules are typically used at intervals to highlight totals and subtotals (see Figure 5.5). But, in general, an extra line space or half-line space does more to break a table into manageable chunks than a rule does.

Tables set into text are typically bounded at the top and bottom by rules. In narrow columns, a 1-point rule will suffice, with 2- and 3-point rules being better balanced for wider measures. Rules inside the table (such as the one under the headings) should be lighter than the exterior rules.

Leaders are rarely used in informational tables, but they are commonly used in other tabular matter, such as in tables of contents, where the leaders connect two pieces of information that are pushed flush against opposite margins. For more on leaders, see Rules, Boxes, and Underscores in Chapter 2.

Characteristics of Popular Roses

Common Name	Coloration		Hardiness	
	Predominant Color	Secondary Color	Freeze Resistance	Pest Resistance
Tupelo Beauty	Red	Gold	High	Low
American Glory	Red	Pink	High	Low
Martha's Classic	Peach	Yellow	Low	High
Lady Godiva	Pink	—	High	High
Pride of Washington	Burgundy	Red	Low	Low
World's Fair	White	—	Low	Low

Characteristics of Popular Roses

Common Name	Coloration		Hardiness	
	Predominant Color	Secondary Color	Freeze Resistance	Pest Resistance
Tupelo Beauty	Red	Gold	High	Low
American Glory	Red	Pink	High	Low
Martha's Classic	Peach	Gold	Low	High
Lady Godiva	Pink	—	High	High
Pride of Washington	Pink	Red	Low	Low
World's Fair	White	—	Low	Low

Figure 5.4
Even flush-left copy can benefit from visual centering. In the upper table, everything is set flush left, except for the centered straddle heads. This makes the whole table seem to lean to the left.

In the lower version, the headings have been nudged to the right so they appear better centered under the straddle heads and rules. In addition, the columns below the headings have been indented by an additional en that makes the whole table appear balanced.

First-Half Sales by Division, 1991 vs. 1990

	1st Quarter		2nd Quarter	
	1990	**1991**	**1990**	**1991**
OEM Sales				
Eastern region	$ 617,995	$ 788,500	$ 694,605	$ 880,005
Midwest region	746,831	677,498	529,775	671,774
Southern region	553,880	995,640	901,442	705,644
Western region	1,876,034	2,880,769	1,705,970	998,777
Total	**$3,794,740**	**$5,342,407**	**$3,831,792**	**$3,256,200**
Retail Sales				
Eastern region	$ 26,995	$ 38,960	$ 35,332	$ 36,719
Midwest region	56,831	58,422	61,666	66,044
Southern region	117,051	121,942	112,545	115,528
Western region	206,774	286,008	210,115	210,773
Total	**$ 407,651**	**$ 505,332**	**$ 419,658**	**$ 429,064**
Total Sales	**$4,202,391**	**$5,847,739**	**$4,251,450**	**$3,685,264**

Figure 5.5

Another complex table:

- The dollar signs—which appear only in the first tab cycles in each section and in the "Total" lines—have been vertically aligned using figure spaces. This alignment is dictated by the widest amount in both sections, so that the dollar signs line up neatly throughout the whole table.
- Both the straddle heads and the year headings have been optically centered by moving them to the left.
- Half-line spaces have been added above the "Total" lines to emphasize them.
- Subheadings in the stub column have been indented one en.
- All the numerical entries have been set flush-right, which has the same effect as decimal alignment in this case.
- Boldface has been used to create a sense of hierarchy in the table, attracting the eye to the "Total" lines. The "grand total" line gets the additional emphasis of hairlines, a common treatment for the "bottom line" in financial tables.
- The clear title makes it immediately obvious what the table is about. The reader can start analyzing the information immediately, rather than first having to figure out what's going on.

Table Miscellany

Don't decimal-align unrelated numbers. When *$100.25* is stacked in a column over *.005 mm,* the entries should align flush-left or centered, but not along their decimal points.

Don't kern numbers in tables. This causes numbers stacked in columns to fall out of alignment (see Kerning in Chapter 1).

Don't use old-style numbers in tables. Old-style numbers don't all base-align, and not all are the same height. In tables—especially financial tables—this creates a disorderly alignment.

Don't use ditto marks. When a tabular entry in a column is the same as in the tab cycle above it, simply repeat the data.

In tables, use commas for numbers over 1,000.

When used in tables, the dollar sign ($) should appear only in the first tab-cycle entry in each column and not again until the total or subtotal line. Entries in intervening cycles should be set as simple numbers.

The dollar signs in the first tab cycle and the total line should align vertically. When two amounts are of different lengths, the dollar sign on the shorter one may be several figure spaces removed from the number itself (see Figure 5.5). If your program doesn't offer figure spaces, set normal numerals (they're all the same width) and specify them as reverse type, which makes them invisible.

Avoid rotated heads, except where many columns are needed. When space is tight, it's tempting to turn column headings on their side to conserve space. Save this as a last resort, as rotated text is difficult to read. When setting rotated headings, set them at a 45-degree angle rather than at a right angle to the text in the tab entries below them (see Figure 5.6).

Income, Month-by-Month

Income Source	January	February	March	April	May	June	July	August	September	October	November	December
Circulation												
New subscriptions	33,200	37,895	29,995	38,965	21,440	27,755	36,625	33,035	38,540	51,760	54,005	58,445
Subscription renewals	5,765	4,315	5,900	6,005	7,900	8,100	10,675	11,765	14,450	17,200	19,655	22,750
Advertising												
Display ads	98,875	94,005	99,220	91,750	86,655	94,050	96,235	99,530	89,545	101,550	103,335	112,650
Directory ads	42,400	38,650	38,675	32,665	38,330	36,665	38,115	36,285	42,555	47,510	51,435	56,055
Classifieds	16,345	11,205	14,000	13,435	15,385	18,945	16,050	14,225	18,350	21,885	24,775	27,555
Inserts	9,500	8,540	9,050	9,855	10,530	11,235	14,335	17,025	18,435	24,445	27,005	31,950
In-the-bag inserts	11,115	10,750	13,655	14,960	18,995	18,665	18,905	15,220	17,550	19,405	23,310	30,055
Seminar subscriptions	55,870	42,110	48,335	44,945	48,885	44,225	44,445	48,930	51,050	54,055	58,445	61,555
Book club sales	22,605	25,675	22,775	28,705	26,650	27,250	29,055	25,540	28,400	31,910	33,295	36,100
Licensing fees	5,000	5,000	5,000	2,500	2,500	5,000	7,500	5,000	7,500	10,000	12,500	15,000
Reprint fees	150	750	550	175	1,050	1,550	850	150	600	775	1,250	1,700

Figure 5.6
When space is tight, rotated heads can be helpful, as long as the text isn't very complex. Also, in this table, half-line spaces have been added between the categories listed in the stub column to make the table easier to read. If more vertical space were available, every line could receive an extra half-line space, with a full line space or line-space-and-a-half between categories.

The commas in the numbers—standard in tables—make the data easier to read.

Preparing an Electronic Manuscript

The biggest practical benefit of an electronic manuscript—such as one prepared with a word processor—is that it never has to be retyped from scratch. It can be edited, altered, dismantled, or merged with other documents, but the words you typed once need never be typed again. This chapter explains how you can specify the *format* of a document—its layout, its typography, its use of special typeset characters—so that, like the text, it also won't have to be reworked from scratch in the future. This can save a lot of time, especially when documents travel from computer to computer and from program to program, an itinerary that's increasingly common in office and publishing environments.

Typically, a document isn't completely created from start to finish within one program or even on one kind of computer. In many offices, for example, text is word processed on IBM PC compatible computers and sent to Apple Macintoshes to be composed into finished pages. Likewise, even if your workgroup all use the same kind of computers, text created in a word processing program is often composed into pages using a separate page makeup or typesetting program. In these cases, the original manuscript has to be created with portability in mind, so that formatting and typographical instructions can travel along with the keystrokes as part of the manuscript.

This gives writers control over the form of the document and saves the page makers extra formatting work.

Even if you work by yourself, or if all of your workgroup use the same word processor to write and create finished pages, portability is still an issue—portability over time. This year's price lists, promotional materials, employee handbooks, and expense forms may all be reused next year, but with new designs. When properly prepared, all these documents can move from computer to computer, program to program, and year to year, and still be reformatted with ease.

ASCII

When you prepare a manuscript for an incompatible computer or program, or when the target computer is unknown, you should produce your manuscript in a universally recognizable file format. A writer preparing a manuscript for an unspecified publisher would work this way. So would an author who posts a manuscript on an electronic bulletin board that can be read by any kind of computer. Most computers and programs need formatting instructions written in their own particular way.

Although richer text formats are being developed, today the common language of all computers is *ASCII* (pronounced *ASS-key*, for *American Standard for Computer Information Interchange*), which is internationally recognized. ASCII works by assigning the numbers 0–127 to the most commonly used printing characters. Some of the numbers are also assigned to some characters used in computer programming and a few basic page and computer commands, such as Tab and Carriage Return. In an ASCII file, all computers will recognize that the number 65 represents a capital *A* and that 112 is a lowercase *p*.

On the printed page, ASCII gives you less than 100 printable characters. These generally include everything you see on your keyboard, including the characters accessible with or without the shift key held down (see Figure 6.1). By comparison, a standard typographic font contains over 200 characters.

ASCII Number	Character	ASCII Number	Character	ASCII Number	Character
32	(space)	64	@	96	`
33	!	65	A	97	a
34	"	66	B	98	b
35	#	67	C	99	c
36	$	68	D	100	d
37	%	69	E	101	e
38	&	70	F	102	f
39	'	71	G	103	g
40	(	72	H	104	h
41	)	73	I	105	i
42	*	74	J	106	j
43	+	75	K	107	k
44	,	76	L	108	l
45	-	77	M	109	m
46	.	78	N	110	n
47	/	79	O	111	o
48	0	80	P	112	p
49	1	81	Q	113	q
50	2	82	R	114	r
51	3	83	S	115	s
52	4	84	T	116	t
53	5	85	U	117	u
54	6	86	V	118	v
55	7	87	W	119	w
56	8	88	X	120	x
57	9	89	Y	121	y
58	:	90	Z	122	z
59	;	91	[	123	{
60	<	92	\	124		
61	=	93	]	125	}
62	>	94	^	126	~
63	?	95	_	127	(delete)

Figure 6.1

This is a list of the ASCII characters 32–127, which are universally recognized by computer systems and text processing programs. They correspond to the so-called *low-bit* ASCII characters printed on most computer and typewriter keyboards. The numbers 0–31 are used for program commands and instructions, including keyboard commands such as *Return*.

The numbers 128–255 represent the *high-bit* ASCII characters, but there is no universal agreement on which characters should be assigned to these numbers. In most desktop publishing programs they are used for accented characters and common typographical characters such as opening and closing quotation marks (" ") and dashes.

How to Prepare an ASCII, or "Text-Only," Manuscript

When preparing an ASCII manuscript, it's important not to use any characters other than those for which there is an assigned number (see Figure 6.2). When the computer cannot read or identify a character or command, it will ignore it or insert a "null" character as a placeholder in the manuscript. This is often the underscore (_) character.

When you save a document that you've created in your word processor, the program won't automatically save it as an ASCII file; it will save it in the program's own file format. For an ASCII file to be universally readable, it has to be written to disk in a specific way. Your program should give you several options for how a file can be saved to disk. You should specify ASCII or *text only*, which is a plain, if somewhat vague, way of specifying an ASCII file. For your future reference, it's useful to name the file in such a way that you can easily recognize it's been saved in ASCII format.

Formatting an ASCII Manuscript

While producing the manuscript, you may prefer to use your word processor's own file format. This enables you to partially format the document as you prepare it, specifying, for instance, line and paragraph indents, margins, line spacing, and font selection. This formatting makes it easier to work on the manuscript, and gives you good-looking printouts as you develop the manuscript. When you finally save the file in ASCII format, all this formatting will be stripped away. The presence of the formatting won't affect how the ASCII file is created—it simply doesn't make it into the ASCII file because the only formatting commands in the ASCII command set are Tab and Carriage Return.

Don't worry about preserving paragraph indents. Carriage returns in an ASCII file are the universal signal for paragraph endings, so the receiving program can convert them back into paragraph indents as needed. However, you should note that *line-ending commands* also called *soft carriage returns* (which some word processors use to

<chapter head>Chapter 4
<chapter title>The Early Venetian Types
<subline>The works of Nicholas Jenson and Manutius Aldus set the stage for contemporary typographic forms.
<chapter open>Before the end of the 15th century, the development of typography had shifted from Germany to Italy, particularly Venice. There, Nicholas Jenson introduced the typeset letterforms that we still use today.
<text>Jenson's types were based on the lettering used by the church in Rome, hence the name <ital>roman <roman>was used to describe types of this style. In 1501, Aldus Manutius (born Aldo Manuzio), also working in Venice, introduced a new style of type based on the popular nonecclesiastical handwriting of the day. It was inclined to the right and took up less room on the page than roman types, enabling Aldus to save printing costs by reducing the number of pages in his books. Aldus dubbed this typeface <ital>italic.
<subhead 1>The Development of Bembo
<para 1>One of Aldus's most enduring designs was a type he created for a book by Cardinal Bembo of Venice. This face has been adapted and copied over the centuries, and contemporary versions are still very popular for book work.

Figure 6.2
This tagged manuscript consists only of ASCII keystrokes. The only formatting is in carriage returns to break lines at the ends of paragraphs. The tags, enclosed in angle brackets (< >), are translated by a type composition program into appropriate formatting commands. Once these tags have been defined in terms of what typographic formatting they represent, the entire manuscript can be printed in the appropriate format at the push of a button. Even if the design of the document changes, the original manuscript and its tags never need additional editing.

break a line without starting a new paragraph) are not in the ASCII character/command set. Avoid using them when creating files that will be saved in ASCII format. How to include non-ASCII characters (such as dashes and opening and closing quotation marks) in an ASCII manuscript is covered in Search and Replace Formatting Strategies in this chapter.

ASCII manuscripts should be *tagged* so they can be easily formatted later (see Tags, Style Sheets, and Generic Markup in this chapter). The recipient of the manuscript can remove the tags easily with a search-and-replace operation if they're not wanted.

Tabs in ASCII

When using the Tab key, keep in mind that the Tab command itself will be maintained in the ASCII file, but not the definition of the depth of the tab indent. The computer that reads the file will set your tabs to whatever it uses as a *default* (or preset) tab value. It's best, then, not to try to create complex tab alignments in an ASCII file.

Where alignment is important, such as in tables, create the text in a spreadsheet, if possible, and save the file in *delimited ASCII* format. This format marks each tab position with an ASCII character (typically a comma) that acts as a delimiter—a boundary marker between tabs. The receiving program rebuilds the tab fields by converting each marker back into a tab command. If necessary, you can also edit a delimited ASCII file in your word processor. Here again the tabs are preserved but their exact spacing is lost and will have to be redefined on the receiving computer. In text tables that you create with your word processor, keep the number of tab columns to a minimum and leave generous spaces between tab columns. This will make it easier for the receiving program to replicate the alignment you've intended.

Tags, Style Sheets, and Generic Markup

The more universally readable you want your manuscript to be, the less typographic formatting, such as specifying typeface, type size, line spacing, indent size, etc., it can include. The epitome of this is an ASCII file (see ASCII above). At the other extreme, compatible programs using the same kind of computer can easily pass documents back and forth without altering the typographic formatting. In any case, though, it's generally to your benefit to process a manuscript's typographic form separately from its textual content.

The best way to do this is with document *tags* and *style sheets*. A tag is a label—a series of keystrokes written directly in the manuscript, such as <*heading*>—that identifies a structural part of the document. A style sheet, in turn, is a directory of typographic definitions for each of these labels. The tag says to the program "This is a heading," and the style sheet says "This is what a heading should look like." When a word processor or page makeup program comes across a tag in a manuscript, it refers to the style sheet and automatically carries out the appropriate formatting instructions. In this system, each structural element in your manuscript—paragraphs, captions, footnotes, etc.—is preceded by an identifying tag (see Figure 6.2). Tags are set off from the surrounding text by *delimiters*, characters such as angle brackets. The delimiters say to the program, "The text inside these characters is a command to you, it is not part of the manuscript." These tags don't contain any formatting instructions, nor will they appear on the final page. They merely identify page elements that will receive some unique formatting treatment.

Generally, only the first of a series of identically formatted text elements, such as the text paragraphs in a book, has to be tagged. When creating your style sheets (see below) you can instruct your program to continue formatting based on one tag until another tag is encountered. This eliminates having to tag every single paragraph within a document or every item in a list.

Any text processing program can create tags—they're keystroked into the manuscript just like the rest of the text. Style sheets, by comparison, are a program's way of carrying out formatting instructions, so each program has its own specific way of creating style sheets. Style sheets from one program generally will not work with any other. Depending on the capability of the program, these instructions can define simple typographic format or complete page layouts, including type sizes, font changes, column widths, and even positions of graphics and charts. Within this system, if a design changes, or if the manuscript is included in another document of different design, the manuscript itself need not be touched. Only the formatting definitions in the style sheet have to be altered, which takes much less time than reformatting the entire manuscript by hand. Changing a style sheet definition creates *global* changes in the manuscript. Changing the definition of how a heading should look automatically changes all the headings in the manuscript. The longer the document, then, the more time tagging will save you.

Because the tags themselves carry no formatting information, one set of tags can be used for many document designs. Likewise, entire document designs can be stored in the form of style sheets, and new designs can easily be created by editing existing style sheets. This means that a writer creating a tagged manuscript effectively formats the document even though the specifics of the final design haven't been decided yet.

Style sheets can be used to format a document automatically or manually. Automatic formatting is useful when importing word-processed files into page makeup programs. In this process, the receiving program reads the tags as it imports the manuscript and carries out all the formatting instructions as it places the text on the page.

If you have an untagged document, you can also manually format it by using a style sheet. In most word processing and page makeup programs, you can display on screen a menu of tag names associated with a particular style sheet. To apply the formatting represented by these tags, you select a passage of text and designate the style sheet tag you'd like to use with it. All of the formatting commands defined in that tag definition are then applied simultaneously. When using a mouse, this process can be performed quickly: click on the text element, click on the tag name, and then move on to the next text element. For a typical text paragraph, one click of the mouse can replace a dozen or more individual formatting moves to establish typeface, line spacing, line and word spacing, measure, etc.

Once your manual formatting is completed, you can have your program create a tagged version of the manuscript, in which all of the applied tags appear in the text. This is useful if the manuscript becomes part of another document or is reformatted in another program, such as a page makeup program.

Ideally, your entire workgroup (or you working alone) should use only one set of tags for all documents. You can build a library of style sheets for all the documents you produce so that old designs can be reused or recycled in slightly modified versions. The word processing department, then, could use one style sheet for preparing manuscripts that serves their programs and their work procedures particularly well. That identically tagged manuscript could then be sent to the page makeup department where another style sheet is used to format the manuscript as a newsletter, report, or brochure. The key to successful tagging is keeping the tag names consistent and simple.

Whenever text is created in one program and converted into final pages in another program, tagging can save time, whether you're working by yourself or as part of a group. The same is true when the parts of a document are created by several authors, as in a journal or newsletter. In these cases, the structural consistency of everyone's contributions can be assured by using the same set of tags, and the work of the person assembling the pages is much easier. The writers can therefore focus on the content of their work without having to worry about its eventual design.

Design and production staffs also benefit, because the repetitive formatting work can be automated if the tagging is done in the writing and editorial process. Designers can also help define the structure of the material to help authors and editors organize and tag the information to follow a specific design.

As long as editorial personnel don't introduce structural elements (and tags) that aren't accounted for in the design—for instance, adding a third level of subheadings to a planned two—the manuscript can be prepared well before the design specifications are finalized. In addition to cutting formatting time, tagging also ensures design consistency by eliminating formatting errors.

SGML

To develop style sheets and document tags you should identify every text element in a document that may have its own unique specifications, such as title, subtitle, byline, caption, headings, first-level subheadings, second-level subheadings, and so on. A complete list of parts of a document can be found in the *Standard Generalized Markup Language*, or *SGML*. SGML lists and describes every conceivable text element that might appear in a document. Its value is that it can serve as a basis for your own tagging scheme, and save you time in analyzing your own documents to create tag names. Even if you choose to use your own labels instead of SGML names, the SGML catalogue is a useful starting point to describe the anatomy of any document. (See the glossary for further information.)

Tagging Styles and Strategies

For tags to be read correctly by the formatting program, they must be distinguishable from the text they're embedded in. For this reason, tag names are flanked front and back by distinctive characters called *delimiters*. They tell the program reading them, "This is where the tag name starts . . . and this is where it ends." The program will then read the tag as an instruction, not as part of your manuscript.

The delimiters used most commonly by text processing programs are angle brackets (< >), but different formatting programs may use characters such as braces ({ }) and brackets ([ ]). If the manuscript isn't being prepared for use with a specific program, it's not important which characters are used as delimiters, as long as their role in the manuscript is clear. Parentheses, for instance, don't make good delimiters because they're so commonly used for other purposes. If the program that reads your tagged manuscript uses delimiters other than the ones you've used, a simple search-and-replace procedure can substitute theirs for yours.

If the tags you produce are for a particular program, create tags that conform to the syntax of that program. This includes the type of delimiter you use, what characters you can and can't use in tag names, and how long tag names can be.

Here are some rules for creating manuscript tags:

- The best tag names are those whose meanings are clear to the keyboarder, such as *subhead2* rather than *SH2*.
- It's better to have too many tag names than too few. If the formats of two text elements differ in even the most minor way,

give each a unique tag. This prevents you from having to make a lot of minor typographical adjustments later.

- Use your word processor's *macro* capability or *glossary* program for inserting tags into your text. These let you assign a string of characters to a single keystroke, so you can add even a long tag name with the push of a button.

Search and Replace Formatting Strategies for Tagged ASCII Manuscripts

Many desktop publishing programs only apply tags to entire paragraphs and do not allow you to apply a tag to a word or phrase within a paragraph. Nevertheless, there are many word- and character-level formatting instructions that the preparer of a generically coded manuscript may want to pass along to the person or program that will eventually format it. In documents saved in ASCII format, these include:

- Important font changes (such as a word that must be italicized, or a typewriter-style quote that must be italicized to form a prime)
- Fractions (to make sure 1/2 is formatted to become $^{1}/_{2}$)
- Characters that are not in the ASCII character set (such as dashes and accented characters)
- Em dashes, which are typically represented in ASCII files as consecutive hyphens

For these and other cases, you need a standard way to relate these instructions to the person or program reading the manuscript. You can use alternate delimiters for these nonstandard tags. Or you can precede the characters that need special attention with a combination of ASCII characters that won't be confused with text, such as ## or ??. The person receiving the document can then search for these flags and take appropriate action. Because these are nonstandard tags, they will be incorrectly interpreted by the receiving program. There-fore, it's important to alert the recipient of the manuscript to the existence and definitions of these tags. Converting them may have to be done manually.

When tagging information within a paragraph, use two delimiters to flank the material you want to be specially formatted. This eliminates any confusion about where the special formatting should begin and end. For example, you could use them to clearly delineate words should be italicized. Backslashes (\\ ) could indicate "italics on" and regular slashes (//) could indicate "italics off." Some programs, particularly code-driven typesetting programs, can be instructed to look for these custom character codes and convert them automatically into the typographic formatting you've specified.

Likewise, some programs will automatically convert a slash flanked by numbers (e.g., 1/4) into a built fraction ($\frac{1}{4}$), but only if the conversion is allowed at the moment. Controlling when this automatic conversion takes place can prevent, for example, the phone number 415/555-1212 from being converted into a fraction. Flagging the 1/4 on both sides (::1/4;; for instance) enables such a program to replace the first flag (::) with an "allow fraction-building" command and the second flag (;;) with a "disallow fraction-building" command. An on/off command like this is called a *toggle* and reflects a basic rule of computer typography: If you turn it on, remember to turn it off.

Quotation Marks in ASCII Files

The proper conversion of quotation marks can be a problem. Not all programs offer "smart-quote" conversion utilities, which automatically convert all typewriter-style quotation marks into typographical opening and closing quotation marks.

Some programs analyze the characters and/or spaces flanking a neutral, typewriter-style quote to determine if it should be translated into an opening (") or closing (") quote. Generally, if a neutral double quotation mark is preceded by a word space, it is an opening quote, and when it is followed by a word space it is almost always a closing quote. Similarly, if a double quote is followed by a character, it is almost always an opening quote, and if it is preceded by a character, it is almost always a closing quote.

But there are exceptions: Quotations inside parentheses, single quotes inside double quotes, and quotes that precede or follow an em dash can cause problems. Typewriter-style quotes used to denote feet and inches can also be a problem. Most "smart-quote" converters are programmed to handle these exceptions, but not all of them catch all possible problems. Whatever conventions you adopt for representing quotation marks, when creating ASCII manuscripts that contain a lot of quotation marks, or where typewriter-style quotes are used in nontraditional ways, it's important to alert the recipients of your manuscript to this fact and to provide them with a translation guide.

Polishing the Manuscript

Before your manuscript can be considered finished, it should be run through a spelling checker and then proofread by another person. There's no substitute for a human proofreader.

If the final version of your manuscript is to be an ASCII document, it should be proofread after being saved in ASCII format, because any non-ASCII characters accidentally used in the original version may disappear or be mistranslated in the conversion process. In addition, you should use your program's search and replace utility to look for errors or oversights, including:

- Multiple word spaces
- Untagged elements
- Unflagged fractions
- Unflagged special characters (such as accented characters or en dashes)
- Font changes
- Extra carriage returns

Glossary

absolute units Measurements such as picas and points, whose values are constant, regardless of the size of the type in which they're used. See *relative units*.

algorithmic hyphenation Computer hyphenation based on logical analysis of words rather than on a dictionary.

ascent line The imaginary line to which the ascending letters (such as *l* or *h*) of a given typeface reach.

ASCII A computer communication standard that applies the numbers 0–127 to common keyboard characters and program commands.

automatic kerning Adjustment of the spaces between individual pairs of letters performed automatically during hyphenation and justification.

base alignment Alignment of characters on a common baseline.

baseline The imaginary line upon which a line of type appears to sit.

bounding box The imaginary box in which each typeset character exists. Vertically, the bounding box encompasses the distance from just above the ascent line to just below the descent line and corresponds to the type's point size. Horizontally, it encompasses the width of the character itself plus the character's side bearings and is equivalent to the character's set width.

Also, the imaginary box in which a block of text exists within a page composition program.

bottom-align To arrange type or graphic elements so that their lowest reaching parts align on a common horizontal line. Also, to align blocks of type so their last lines share a common baseline.

call-out A piece of display type, such as an enlarged quote, used as a graphic or attention-getting device in text.

capital line The imaginary line that coincides with the tops of the capital letters in a given typeface.

center on body To vertically center a character on an axis midway between the ascent and descent lines of a passage of type. Parentheses and brackets typically center on the body of the text with which they are set.

center on cap height To vertically center a character on an axis midway between the baseline and the capital line.

center on x-height To vertically center a character on an axis midway between the baseline and the mean line.

character set The complete set of letters, numerals, punctuation marks, and symbols that constitute a font.

character width The width of a typeset letter, as measured in relative units.

color In typography, the overall texture of typeset text created by the balance of black ink against the white background of the page. Type that is alternately set tight and loose on the same page is said to lack consistent color.

compound rule Two rules used together, usually as a border, and often varying in weight. See *Scotch rule.*

condensed A version of a typeface that has been designed to be narrower than the regular version.

coupon rule Typographic term for a dashed or dotted line, typically used as a border.

c/lc Abbreviation for *capitals and lowercase.* Same as u/lc.

default In a computer program, the preset specifications that are in effect when the program is started.

delimited ASCII A form of ASCII text in which tabs or the divisions between database fields are indicated by a character (often a comma) called a delimiter.

delimiters Characters in a manuscript that are used as signals to a computer program and are not read as a part of the manuscript text. Delimiters may signal a formatting code or identify structural elements of a document.

descent line The imaginary line to which the descending characters (such as *j* or *y*) of a typeface reach.

dingbat A decorative typographic character used as a highlight or border element.

discretionary hyphen A hyphen that you can add in a text processing program to prompt the program to break a line. The hyphen only prints if it appears at the end of a line. Also called a *soft hyphen.*

down style Display-type or headline style in which only the first letter of the text is capitalized. See *up style.*

em A typographic measurement equal in width to the point size in which it is used. In 14-point type an em is 14 points wide.

en A typographic measurement equal in width to half the point size of the type in which it is used. In 14-point type an en is 7 points wide.

em dash A dash that is one em wide. It is used as a separating form of punctuation, akin to parentheses or a semicolon.

en dash A dash that is one en wide. It is used as a connecting form of punctuation, typically to connect ranges of numbers (e.g., 20–40).

em space A fixed space that is one em wide.

en space A fixed space that is one en wide.

exception dictionary In text processing programs, a supplementary dictionary that you create to include words not in the program's own hyphenation dictionary or words that are improperly handled by its hyphenation algorithm. Also called a supplementary dictionary.

expanded A version of a typeface that has been designed to be wider than the regular version of that face.

figure space A fixed space that is the same width as the numerals within a typeface. It is commonly used as a placeholder to align numbers in tabular matter.

first-line indent   An indent that occurs only on the first line of a paragraph.

fixed spaces   Typographic spaces that unlike a word space are not altered during hyphenation and justification. Fixed spaces include em, en, thin, and figure spaces.

flush left   Text set so that the left-hand ends of all lines of type abut the margin. The term implies a ragged-right margin.

flush right   Text set so that the right-hand ends of all lines of type abut the margin. The term implies a ragged-left margin.

folio   A page number. The term is also used to describe the total page count of a document. In addition, *folio* is used to describe the size of a book whose pages are formed by folding a larger sheet of paper in half.

font   The physical form of a typeface. In computer typography, a font is a set of mathematical descriptions of the shapes of the letters of a typeface, stored as programming code on a disk or other storage medium.

fraction bar   An angled line used to build typeset fractions. It differs in weight, angle, and spacing characteristics from the slash character found on most keyboards.

grid   The underlying structure of a page, consisting of nonprinting guidelines that determine the placement of columns of type, display type, and other page elements.

grid line   A non-printing horizontal line on a typeset page that acts as a vertical alignment guide for text and graphics.

gutters   Vertical bands of open space that separate columns of type and tabular columns. In book work, the binding margins of the page.

hairline   A thin typographic rule, less than one-quarter point thick.

halftone   An image—such as a photograph—prepared for printing by being converted into an array of dots of varying size. These dots against the white background of the page create the optical illusion of gradations of color—half tones—especially when the dots are very small.

hang line   A grid line used as a top-alignment guide for text or graphic elements.

hanging indent   An indent characterized by one line set to full measure and subsequent lines being indented from the left-hand margin by a consistent amount.

hard hyphen   A hyphen that is a permanent part of a manuscript, as keyed in using the hyphen key.

hyphenation and justification (h&j)   The set of procedures a computer program uses to fit type into lines. It consists of counting the cumulative widths of the characters on each line, adjusting word and letter spacing, and hyphenating words if necessary to fit an optimum number of letters on each line.

indent on text   A hanging indent whose depth is based on the width of a passage of typeset text.

jump line   An instruction to the reader indicating that the text continues on, or is continued from, another page.

justified   In reference to margin treatment, lines that completely fill the specified measure, creating smooth margins.

kerning   The adjustment of the spaces between particular letter pairs to compensate for their incongruent shapes and restore spacing consistent with surrounding text.

kerning table   A list of pairs of letters and the kerning adjustments that should be made to them, used by a composition program to automatically kern text.

leader   A string of identical characters—most commonly periods—used to connect related pieces of text across a page or table.

leading   Pronounced *ledding,* the distance between lines of type, as measured from the baseline of one line to the baseline of the preceding line.

letterspace   To letterspace is to exaggerate the spacing between letters in a line of type, usually for display purposes.

line space   A blank line of type set on the same leading as the type above and below it, typically created by hitting the Return key.

line spacing The term used by most word processing programs to describe leading.

logic-based hyphenation See *algorithmic hyphenation.*

loose line A line in which the composition software has had to stretch word and/or letter spaces beyond specified limits.

macro A series of keystrokes and/or program commands enacted by a single keystroke or command.

manual kerning Adjustment by hand of the spacing between particular pairs of letters, often necessary in large display type to achieve consistent spacing.

margin treatment How lines of type fill the measure, hence how the margins of the text column are formed. For example, lines that fill the measure completely are called *justified,* and lines that abut the right margin but fall short of the right margin are called *flush left.*

mean line An imaginary line that corresponds to the tops of the nonascending lowercase letters, as exemplified by the letter *x.*

measure The line length specified for a passage of type, thus the column width of a block of type.

monospaced typeface A typeface such as Courier, all of whose letters have the same width. See *proportionally spaced typeface.*

non-breaking space In computer type composition, a space that is the same width as a word space but is not a legal place to break a line. Two words or characters linked by a non-breaking space will always appear on the same line together.

old style figures Numerals that do not all base align and are not all the same height.

orphan A short paragraph fragment that appears at the top of a column or page.

outdent Back-formation of the word *indent,* used to describe a hanging indent in which the first line of the paragraph extends out beyond the left-hand column margin.

page description language A programming language, such as PostScript, whose vocabulary can describe all of the printed events on a page, including type, line art, and screened graphics. Page layout programs use page description languages so that all page elements can be described and assembled electronically, eliminating the need for hand paste-up.

paragraph indent   See *first-line indent*.

pi characters   Utility characters outside of the normal character set used for text. Common pi characters include bullets, boxes, stars, and triangles.

pi font   A utility font consisting of pi characters and other useful symbols, such as math and scientific characters.

pica   An absolute typographic measurement traditionally equal to almost one-sixth inch. Contemporary composition programs, such as those based on PostScript, round this off to exactly one-sixth inch.

point   An absolute typographic measurement equal to one/twelfth of a pica.

point size   The size of type, measured as the distance from just above the tallest characters in a typeface (that is, just above the ascent line) to just below the lowest reaching ones (below the descent line).

primes   The angled superior characters used as symbols for minutes/seconds and feet/inches.

proportionally spaced typeface   A font whose characters have unique individual widths. Because letters historically have been drawn with varying widths, proportionally spaced typefaces can reproduce letters in optimally legible designs.

ragged   A margin formed by lines that do not fully fill the measure. See *margin treatment*.

recto   In an open book, newspaper, or magazine, the right-hand page. Recto pages get odd page numbers, or folios.

re-rag   The change in line endings that occurs when text has been edited or typographically respecified. Hand re-ragging may be necessary to fix loose and tight lines and other layout problems.

relative units   Typographical measurements based on the em. Kerning increments, for instance, are tiny fractions of an em. Because the width of an em changes with the point size of the type, measurements and movements expressed in relative units remain proportional as point sizes change.

run-in Describing text elements that immediately follow one another on the same line. The words that are defined in this glossary, for example, are set using a run-in style.

running foot A repeating text element that occurs at the bottom of every page.

running head A repeating text element that occurs at the top of every page.

running indent A right or left indent that is used for a number of lines.

runover The continuation of a line of type that's carried down to begin a new line when the previous line has been filled. Also called a turn line or turnover.

Scotch rule A compound rule made up of one thick and one thin line, commonly used as a border.

set width The width of a character as it appears on the page. The set width of a character may be modified electronically by a composition program to some percentage—narrower or wider—of the character's normal width.

SGML The Standard Generalized Markup Language, a set of identifying labels that describe the structural parts of any document. These labels are used by the originator of a document to label all the parts of a document; the labels are later translated into typographic and page formatting codes. For more information on SGML, contact the Electronic Publishing Special Interest Group (EPSIG), c/o Online Computer Library Center (OCLC), 6565 Frantz Road, Dublin, OH 43017-0702.

side bearings The small slivers of white space on either side of typeset letters that keep them from touching each other when set into lines.

skew An angled margin.

small caps Capital letters that are about two-thirds the size of normal capitals, used for display type and some abbreviations.

smart quote converter A utility in some composition programs for automatically converting typewriter-style quotation marks (") into their typographical equivalents (" ").

soft carriage return A computer line-ending command that starts a new line without starting a new paragraph.

soft hyphen   A hyphen introduced by composition software when fitting type into lines. Also a hyphen prompted by the user of the program when a word fails to hyphenate properly. See *discretionary hyphen*.

space band   A word space.

straddle head   In a table, a heading that acts as an umbrella head over two or more other headings.

stub tab   In a table, the left-most column, in which the subjects being compared are listed.

style sheets   Libraries of formatting commands associated with sets of text identifiers called *tags*. When a composition program encounters such tags, it looks up their meanings in a specified style sheet and automatically formats the document accordingly.

tab field   In typography, a tabular column.

tags   Labels added to an electronic manuscript to identify the structural parts of the document. Tags are read by composition software and converted into formatting commands. See *style sheets*.

text only   Same as ASCII.

thin space   A fixed space whose width can usually be defined within a composition program. The thin space is typically about the same width as a word space.

tight line   A line in which the composition software has had to squeeze word and/or letter spaces beyond specified limits.

tight rag   A ragged margin in which there is little variation between the lengths of the lines. See *wild rag*.

top-align   To position typeset characters of various sizes so that the tops of all the characters align along the same horizontal line. Also, to so position a piece of type relative to a graphic or rule.

tracking   The overall tightness of the spacing within a passage of text. Tracking is typically tightened in display sizes, because in large point sizes type appears too loosely set.

turn line, turnover   See runover.

typeface   A set of characters sharing a common design motif. Typefaces are organized into families consisting of related designs that vary in weight and width, and include roman and italic complements.

u/lc   Abbreviation for upper and lower case. Same as *c/lc*.

underscore   A rule set for emphasis underneath a line of type.

up style   Display or headline text set with all initial capitals, except for articles and short prepositions.

verso   In an open book, newspaper, or magazine, the left-hand page. Verso pages get even page numbers, or folios.

widow   In typography, a short last-line of a paragraph or a short paragraph fragment that appears at the bottom of a page or column.

wild rag   A margin formed by lines whose lengths vary greatly from one another. See *tight rag*.

word space   The space between words as created by the space bar on the keyboard. In most contemporary composition and text processing programs, the width of the word space is defined in the font, but some programs allow you to define the width of the word space yourself.

wrap   In typography, a margin that's shaped around a graphic or another piece of text. Also, the breaking of a line of text when it has grown too long to fit within the measure. In this sense, *re-wrap* is the same as *re-rag*.

x-height   The height of the nonascending lowercase letters in a typeface, as typified by the lowercase *x*.

Index